W9-BVF-485

# *You in Your Kitchen*

ANTINORI

The Danbury Press

WOMAN ALIVE

# You in Your Kitchen

by Dilys Wells

Series Coordinator: John Mason
Design Director: Guenther Radtke
Designer: Roger Hyde
Editor: Mitzi Bales
Research: Marian Pullen
Frances Vargo
Consultants: Beppie Harrison
Jo Sandilands


ISBN: 84 - 382 - 0002 - 8
Depósito Legal: S. S. 890 - 74
Library of Congress
Catalog Card No. 72-85024
**Printed and bound in Spain by**
T.O.N.S.A. and Roner, S. A.
Ctra. de Irún, Km. 12,450.
Fuencarral - Madrid-34.

*This is a book about cooking, rather than a cookbook. Instead of the flat instructions you find in all the recipes you've ever tried to follow, you'll find the reasons behind the directions - and this knowledge will at last free you from blind obedience to a cookbook. Here you will learn what happens in the actual process of cooking, how you can diagnose a failure so as to avoid it next time, what the essential tools of the trade are. Here, too, are a dozen basic recipes with several variations, given with step-by-step photos in full color. Master these, and you can build on them to achieve that casual-but-sure skill of the experienced cook who will try anything. Just as important, your new mastery should help you enjoy cooking more.*

# Contents


The Talented Amateur: Picture Essay 6

1 Starting Out Right 16

2 What Happens When You Cook 36

3 Themes and Variations 56

4 When Things Go Wrong 85

5 New Ways, Old Ways 100

6 Food with a Foreign Accent 117

Tips and Hints & Glossary 129

For Your Bookshelf 144

# The Talented Amateur

Even though housewives don't get paid for their work as chief cook, many are of equal ability to the professional chef. They attain such skill by perseverence, talent, care—and, often, formal study in classes.

**Right:** a visitor to a Victorian cooking school gets a taste of one of the goodies, offered by the proud person who made it.

**Below:** starting a child off early in the kitchen—with patience and love—is a good way to make her enjoy cooking later in life.

**Below:** it may not be all fun, but a school home economics course usually gives a girl a good foundation in the basics of cooking.

**Below right:** some women like to read cookbooks just for the pleasure of it, as well as consulting them for all kinds of information.

**Above:** when adults take a course in cooking, they usually do so because they like to cook, and want to improve their skills.

**Above right:** serving a Swiss fondue at a dinner party is an easy and pleasant way to learn more about food from other countries.

**Right:** men often discover that they enjoy cooking if they get the proper encouragement. Trying pastry is a bold step, indeed.

# More than a Meal

There are some happy times when the food we eat is special in the way it is made and served—certainly more sumptuous than usual, and often reserved just for the occasion. In fact, the meal becomes a feast—and the memory of it can linger long in the mind.

**Left:** when is a picnic not a mere picnic? When, as shown in this painting of Victorian times, it is served like a grand dinner.

**Below:** the young Queen Victoria attends a banquet at the ancient Guildhall in 1837—and the guest list numbers in the hundreds.

**Above left:** Christmas and rich food are practically synonymous. Dickens describes the fun and feasting in *The Christmas Carol.*

**Above:** the elegant restaurant in the exclusive Savoy Hotel was a favorite eating place for London's high society in Edwardian days.

**Below:** the "Festival of the Hungry Ghosts", as celebrated in Hong Kong, calls for luxurious and dainty dishes in great quantity.

**Above:** cake and ice cream and other kinds of food that satisfy a sweet tooth are the order of the day at a child's birthday party.

# Food for Tomorrow

With the world population increasing year by year, the food supply must be stretched to feed more and more people. To do this without destroying the environment, scientists are developing substitutes for meat—which is the biggest source of protein intake—as well as new ways of growing food.

**Below:** the two sticks of kabob on the left in this picture are made of soya, a high protein food that can substitute for meat.

**Above and below:** at the electronic controls of a beef foodlot in Colorado, an operator automatically measures out the proper amount of feed for a tremendous number of cattle.

**Above:** overfishing is making common food fish extinct, so we'll now have to go deeper into the sea for such fish as the grenadier.

**Right:** shown here is a protein food in meal form, synthesized from maize, sorghum, and cottonseed. It can replace meat in a diet.

**Above:** making arid desert land fertile is the formula for producing more food on the Israeli kibbutzim—and it has been working.

**Right:** today there is a bigger trend toward growing the family supply of fresh vegetables and fruit in one's own garden.

# Food Taboos

Over the centuries, food has been closely tied in with mankind's social and religious beliefs. This has given rise to rules and regulations on what may or may not be eaten, and many people give strict adherence to the laws that govern their daily diets.

**Right:** a bloody uprising by Indians against the British in 1857 occurred over a misunderstanding about cartridge grease said to infringe on both Hindu and Muslim food taboos.

**Below:** the cow that is held sacred by Hindus is paraded in honor along the streets.

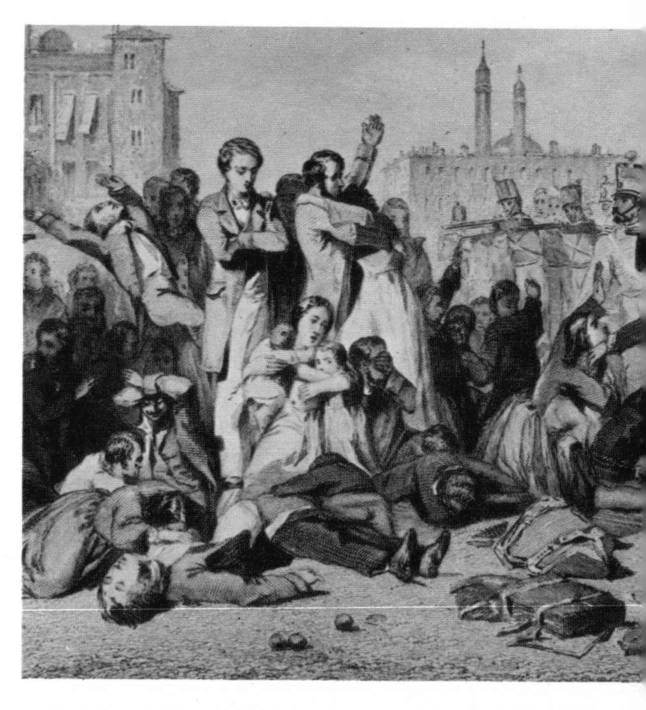

**Right:** a strict Buddhist is also a strict vegetarian. Many of the vegetarian dishes popular today are based on Buddhist recipes.

**Above right:** Catholic families traditionally eat only fish on Fridays. The law on this is now more lenient, but the habit persists.

**Below:** eating in a health food bar helps overcome one of the new food taboos—usually self-imposed—against food additives.

**Right:** orthodox Jews not only keep separate table and kitchen ware for meat and milk dishes, but also change all these at Passover.

# Back to Basics

Less than a hundred years ago, it was common for women to bake all the bread, make all the jams and preserves, and do a large amount of canning. Today, there is a growing tendency—especially among the younger people—to do as our grandparents used to do, and buy far fewer manufactured foods.

**Right:** soon there will be fresh, healthful, and delicious homemade bread on the table of this Canadian farmhouse, as pictured about 65 years ago.

**Below:** the big difference in taste between homemade and bought jams has prompted many moderns to do their own jam making.

**Above:** it can be a happy family affair when there's a vegetable patch in the back yard.

**Above:** the renewed desire for natural foods has popularized health food restaurants.

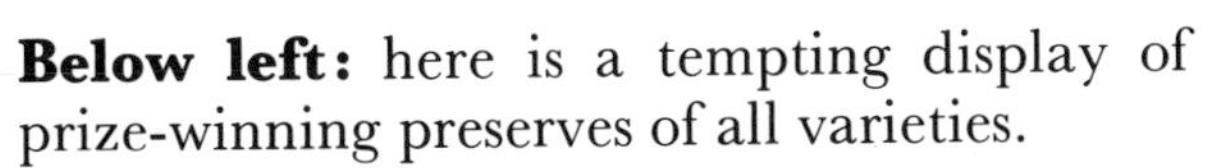

**Below left:** here is a tempting display of prize-winning preserves of all varieties.

**Below:** more people today insist on free-range chickens and eggs for taste and quality.

# Starting Out Right

# 1

Say the word "cooking" to a few women and see what different reactions you get. You probably know someone just like Diana Phipps, who will shudder slightly and say "ugh". She finds it a positive chore to cook. Then there's someone else like Jenny Castigli. She shrugs indifferently and says it's simply another housekeeping activity she takes in her stride. Those like Marion Bloch, though, will light up with enthusiasm. Marion thinks of cooking as a creative art form that helps her make one of the most important contributions to family life.

Whatever your own present attitude to cooking, and whatever your degree of experience in the kitchen, you'll find that a spark of interest in the subject—backed by a good working knowledge of basic techniques—can make cooking a greater pleasure and an easier job. This book is designed to spark your interest and improve your techniques. It will do this by an emphasis on tools, methods, and variations rather than on recipes. So, get set to have fun learning about cooking as a skill and a vocation rather than as a catalog of recipes.

First of all, let's face up to the fact that we are living in a prepackaged society where food's concerned. It's so easy to open a can or a box—and there's so much variety of choice—that many of us take this easy way out. On the other hand, there is an opposite trend, too. Many women—and men as well—are turning to complicated cookery as a form of relaxation. Cooking classes are usually well attended, and glossy cookbooks sell by the million. We want to keep a balance between the sensible use of convenience foods, and the preservation of home cooking as a worthwhile craft. For most of us, complicated gourmet cooking is not a high priority—and needn't be.

Nonetheless, to be able to serve a fine meal, you need both skill and flair. You can acquire the skill with relative ease, and you can develop a flair even if you weren't born with it. You simply need basic knowledge to blend and serve foods that complement one another in flavor, taste, color, and texture. There is great pride in craftsmanship when carefully prepared ingredients are cooked to perfection. There is great joy in transforming raw ingredients into an exquisite meal—one that first pleases the eye, and then the palate. Compliments from guests are as rewarding as medals of honor.

Fortunately, many of us as average cooks get as much—or more—satisfaction when our family tucks into a plain and unpretentious meal with obvious enjoyment. That's the other side of the art of cooking: making the ordinary family meal tasty and satisfying. It may be slightly disappoining if the brood can't tell the difference between the beef Sauerbrauten you spent two days on, or the flavorsome beef stew you pressure cooked in an hour. However, it can't be totally disappointing if they truly enjoy both.

### Budget cooking

Happily, there is no rule that the most expensive ingredients make the best meal. Many world famous dishes are made from inexpensive raw materials, and many mothers throughout the world find that the most popular meals they serve are simple and

Cooking as a creative art depends in part on liking to cook—but a real interest, some care and attention, and a little study can open the doors to culinary mastery for all.

# *Measuring and Mixing It*

Having and using the right tools for cooking not only saves you time and trouble, but also helps you achieve the best possible results. This is especially true of baking, in which measuring and mixing aids play so important a part. To be sure you have what you need for mixing ingredients—whether it's to make a sauce or a cake, a pudding or a pie crust—check the basic equipment illustrated here.

**1** One-pint measuring cup
**2** Measuring spoons
**3** Small, medium, large mixing bowls
**4** Assortment of wooden spoons
**5** Rolling pin
**6** Strainer
**7** Flour sifter
**8** Pastry blender
**9** Rubber scraper
**10** Medium wire whisk
**11** Rotary beater
**12** Measuring cups

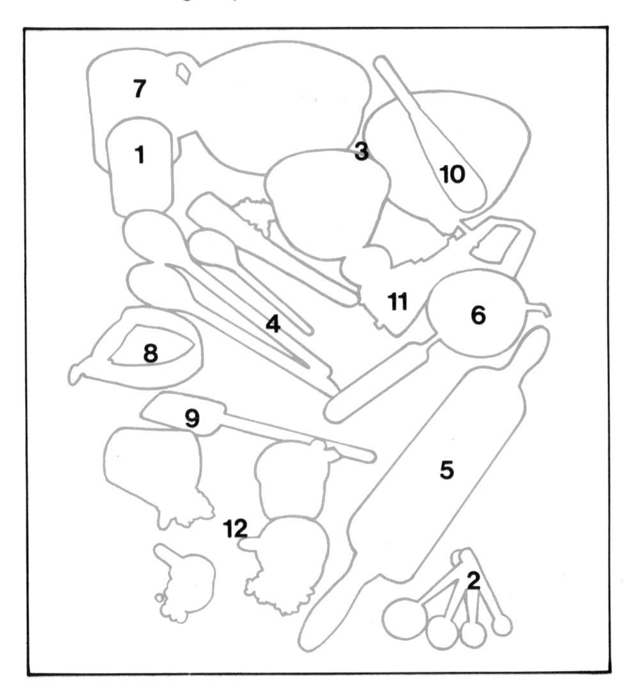


reasonable. When you don't have unlimited funds for shopping—and who does?—you will find that you need to spend more time to produce a good meal. Time is usually the secret ingredient in making a meal that pleases everyone, but still stays within your budget. For example, cheap meats often have a better flavor than the expensive ones, because our meat is priced by its tenderness rather than by its flavor. The cheaper cuts are always tougher, however. You can just flash a tender filet mignon under the broiler, but chuck needs a gentle, lengthy simmering. Take the time to use the suitable tenderizing method of cooking, and your meal of chuck will shine.

It takes a clever cook to make a delicious and nourishing soup from a pound or so of stewing meat, a handful of vegetables, and an imaginative use of herbs. But such cleverness is not beyond most of us, if we have a few tips and guidelines. Helen O'Connor may astound you by serving "Mexican spiced pancakes" made from the leftover chili con carne she brilliantly put to this use. Nothing wrong in your adapting this idea for the day you have only eggs, milk, and leftovers—perhaps chicken à la king instead of chili—in the refrigerator. Ingenuity—not necessarily genius—can transform a few strips of bacon, some eggs, onion, and Swiss cheese into a mouth-watering Quiche Lorraine. (Only the name is a bit fancy; it's a simple unsweetened pastry shell with a custard-like filling of the ingredients named above.)

In these days of high inflation, cooking on almost any budget depends on wise shopping. You already know that that means buying foods in season, when they are at their best and cheapest, and making careful price comparisons in various stores. Radio programs and newspaper articles often give helpful guidance on best food buys at a given time.

## Tools of the Trade

There's an old saying that a craftsman is as good as his tools, and this very much holds true for the cook. Some cooks may work wonders with a couple of sharp knives, a bowl, and a wooden spoon—but it's likely that they

# Cooking It

Right: sturdy, well-balanced saucepans with tight fitting lids make all the difference in cooking, and a heavy frying pan is also a must. Many cooks can get by without a double boiler, but once you've discovered its convenience and usefulness, you'll certainly want one in your kitchen. As for roasts, you'll want both an uncovered and a covered roasting pan to do them exactly to the right turn.

Left: when it comes to choosing saucepans, it's false economy to buy cheap light ones. Get the best quality you can possibly afford.

would save time and energy if they had somewhat more to work with. Others may have a kitchen fully equipped with the latest labor-saving devices, but produce nothing out of the ordinary as cooks. Perhaps they would do better with less equipment and more basic knowledge. The point is to have the proper tools, and to use them right.

The equipment you have should be put to full use to earn its keep. It won't do so if you keep your electric mixer in the back of a cupboard, and its attachments in their unopened boxes, for example. It will only do so if you keep the mixer plugged in on top of your main working surface, ready for instant use. The extra attachments should be kept in a handy drawer. Equipment you don't use just makes clutter—and won't pay for itself besides.

Do you have a Louise Muller among your acquaintances? Louise is hopelessly gadget-minded. She has drawer after drawer of gadgets—all promising to take the hard work out of any chore while producing fancy dainties of all kinds. Yet you know Louise generally serves the plainest broiled chops and baked potatoes. You rightfully suspect that cooks like her get more fun out of buying than using their equipment.

It's not unreasonable to have gadgets, such

**1** Small, medium, and large saucepans with lids
**2** Cast iron frying pan with lid
**3** Covered roasting pan
**4** Large soup kettle
**5** Small casserole
**6** Double boiler
**7** Roasting pan
**8** Pie pan
**9** Pot holders

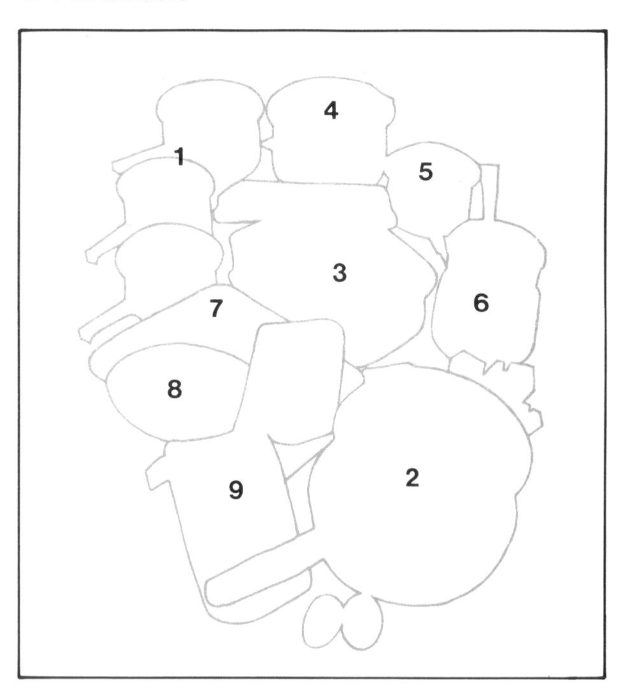

as shredders and choppers, especially if you serve a great many raw salads and like the ingredients finely done. These tools also come in handy for fine shredding in the Chinese style. Remember, though, the Chinese cook doesn't find them in the least essential.

While stressing that you shouldn't go overboard on equipment, we must also say that what you do buy is personal choice. It depends on the kind of you life you lead, and the food you serve. Working wives, for example, may find an automatic range a life saver. With it they can leave the dinner cooking in the oven while they are out at work. Bachelors and single women living in a small apartment may want a quick and simple meal when they come home from work. They may find a pressure cooker, infra red grill, rotisserie, or elec-

# *Baking It*

The smell, the look, the taste of homemade cakes, cookies, and other baked goodies have no equal—and the sharing of home-baked bread is almost a mystical experience. You'll find that you'll have the greatest success in baking if you use the right kind and right size of pans. Here are some recommended basics.

**1** 8-inch layer cake pan
**2** One-pound loaf pan
**3** Two-pound loaf pan
**4** Muffin tin
**5** Cookie sheet
**6** Cooling rack

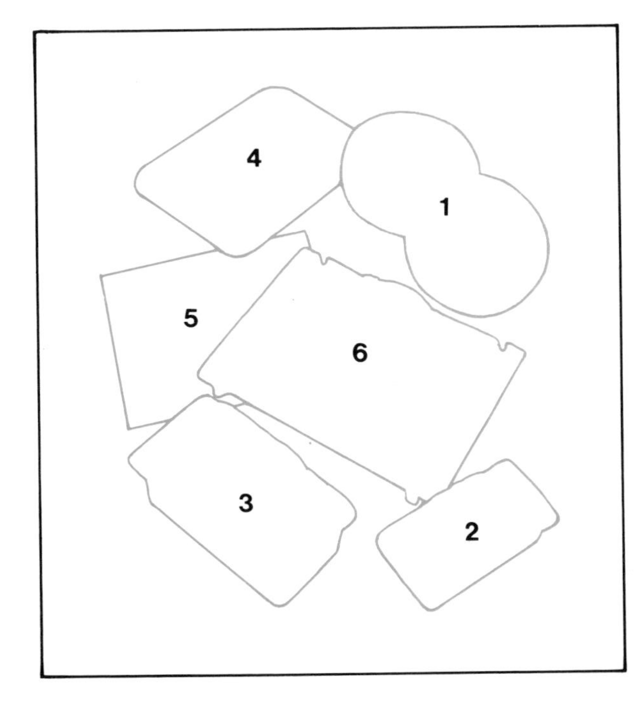


tric frying pan best for their needs. On the other hand, a woman who is at home all day and likes to fuss with food may be just the one to have a heavy duty mixer with all the attachments. Coffee lovers who must have the perfect cup of coffee often make good use of a coffee grinding attachment to their mixer, or a small separate grinder if they have no mixer. Self-ground coffee is not only fresher and more aromatic, but also saves on cost, because coffee is usually cheaper in the bean.

Now let's talk more about basics. Whatever cooking you do, the right tool for the job speeds the work and improves the result. No one will get very far preparing a grapefruit with a carving knife. You need the right size baking pan if your cakes are not to overflow, or come out crisp and thin as a cookie. You cut your peparation time if you have plenty of mixing bowls, if your beaters are both the right size and the right type, if you have enough spatulas, wooden spoons, pancake turners, and ladles. Your finished dish has a professional look if you use an icing set to make Duchesse potatoes, to form a meringue case, to decorate a dessert with rosettes of cream. So the main question is: what is the minimum of proper equipment you need to do a good, or better, job of cooking?

We've already said that some cooks work wonders with almost no equipment, but most cooks can't—and shouldn't. You need certain essentials if you want to run your kitchen efficiently, and also have time left for life outside the kitchen. Let us say that you might be preparing three, or even four, meals a day, with an occasional special dinner thrown in. Your absolute basics are knives, saucepans and casseroles, baking pans, and measuring and mixing utensils. Among these, more than one of a kind is needed. The illustrations show you what the basically well-equipped kitchen should contain: see page 24 for cutting equipment, 20 for cooking utensils, 23 for baking needs, and 19 for measuring and mixing aids.

Say you now know what you need, either as someone starting out fresh, or as someone adding to what is already on hand. How do you get the best type of product, and the best buy for your money? Here are some useful ideas.

### A few hints on buying pots and pans

Look around any large store and you're bound to be impressed by the great variety of cooking equipment on sale. You'll probably also be rather confused about the best ones to buy for your own purposes. A great deal of science has gone into making good quality pans that heat up quickly and evenly without burning food. Attention is also paid to heating efficiency. But how can you tell which saucepan is sturdy and efficient just by looking at it? You can't. So, pick it up. Good pans are always fairly heavy. (Light, flimsy ones may be cheaper, but they make food stick and burn, and they wear out quicker.) A good pan will also have a tight fitting lid. Look carefully at the base. It should be as wide as the burners on your range, because a narrow-based pan will waste fuel.

After these considerations, your best bet is to buy the most expensive pans you can afford. This is not extravagance, but sound investment. Don't be carried away by the color and decoration of the product, however. Many modern designs are so delightful they are hard to resist, but colors and looks are not enough. Often the brightly decorated pots are not as good underneath. Therefore, even if the decorated ones cost the same as plain ones, take the latter.

Cooking utensils are made in a variety of materials, among them aluminum, cast iron, enamel, stainless steel, and copper. Choose according to your own taste, but remember these things: even expensive enamel may chip in time; copper needs to be cleaned every time you use the pan if you want it to stay bright and burnished; cast iron is extremely heavy; nonstick linings are relatively easy to scratch, and this shortens the life of the pan.

### A few hints on buying knives

How can you trim away tough gristle, dice vegetables, or cube meat if your knife barely cuts butter? How can you pare an apple with a butcher knife, or slice a roast with a paring knife? You can't. That's why a sharp knife of the right kind for the job is a cook's best friend.

If you want sharp knives that can easily be kept sharp, tempered steel blades are the first choice. They give the best cutting edge. However, they also discolor quickly, and take a firm scrubbing with wire pads and scouring powder. Stainless steel knives, on the hand, stay shiny and clean a long time, but don't

# *Cutting It*

Good knives are one of the greatest boons to a cook—and a sturdy chopping board to help keep them from getting dull fast. Although tempered steel knives can rust, and so take more care, many prefer them to any others because they can be kept sharp more easily.

**1** 8-inch-blade knife
**2** 6-inch-blade knife
**3** 4-inch-blade knife
**4** Grapefruit knife
**5** Vegetable knife with serrated edge
**6** Bread knife with serrated edge
**7** Knife sharpener
**8** Wooden chopping board

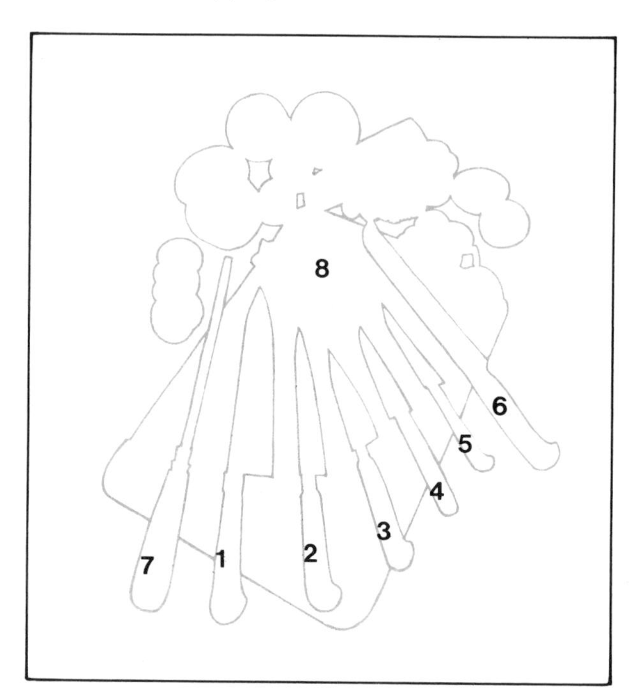


sharpen so well. As for a sharpener, the simplest one is also a very efficient one. It's a rod of abrasive material that looks like a poker and is called a steel. A wall sharpener, a wheel sharpener, or an electric sharpening attachment on your electric mixer are also good.

Whether you decide on tempered or stainless steel knives, buy those with blades firmly

riveted into the handle. Test the knife in your hand for balance. Good knives should be heavy in the hand. A flimsy knife is not an efficient tool because it will tend to fly out of your hand when you're using it rapidly. Price is usually a fairly accurate guide to the quality of a knife. Like in shopping for saucepans, buy the most expensive knives you can afford. No matter how good your knives are to start with, you'll dull them quickly if you chop with them on metal or laminated plastic surfaces. Choose a heavy wooden chopping board to work on—and make it a big one if you cook a lot.

What size of various pieces of equipment should you have? That depends on the number of people you usually cook for. If you have a large family, or entertain large groups regularly—of if you like to do a batch of cooking for freezer storage—you will need larger utensils than if you are cooking for just two or three. However, an extra-large pan and a king-size casserole are always useful even if you only entertain occasionally, and there's also the Thanksgiving turkey to roast. Some things, such as stock, are not worth making in small amounts, so you'll need a large pot for that.

Although more and more women are coming to rely on an electric mixer these days, this kitchen aid is not really practical unless you do a lot of cooking and baking. If you do, though, an all-purpose, heavy duty mixer is a real boon.

The modern all-purpose mixer has a basic engine with a rotary arm to which a wide variety of attachments can be fitted. With them, you can do everything from mixing bread dough to squeezing fresh orange juice to shredding vegetables. For cooking and baking, which usually requires mixing in a bowl, there are whisks, beaters, and dough hooks. In addition, there are such attachments as a blender, juicer, food grinder, coffee grinder, vegetable slicer and shredder, potato peeler, can opener, and knife sharpener. Of course, you won't need all the attachments at once. The bowls and beaters are the first essentials. Remember, stainless steel bowls are better than heat-resistant glass ones, which are inclined to break at the most inconvenient times. Some mixers take bowls of different sizes, and this is an advantage if you are whipping a small amount of expensive cream. There are also mixers made so the bowl rotates as well as the rotary arm. This seems to make mixing quicker and more efficient.

Does the amount of cooking you do justify the amount of money wou would spend on a machine such as this? If you cook for a large family daily, the answer is almost certainly "yes". The attachments can help you prepare large quantities of food quickly. For example, it's no light task to peel and slice enough potatoes for scalloped potatoes to feed six-to-eight hearty appetites. The peeler and slicer

# Useful Odds and Ends

Here are some kitchen aids that you can hardly do without, even if you don't use each and every one of them daily. When you want a corkscrew or a grater, for example, nothing else will do. So check the drawers and pegboard to see that you have these useful odds and ends.

**1** Lemon squeezer
**2** Grater
**3** Can opener
**4** Beer can opener
**5** Corkscrew
**6** Mold
**7** Colander
**8** Kitchen scissors
**9** Potato and vegetable peeler
**10** Pancake turner
**11** Slotted kitchen spoon
**12** Metal kitchen spoon
**13** Metal spatula
**14** Pastry brush
**15** Tongs
**16** Funnel
**17** Meat mallet
**18** Timer
**19** Bulb baster
**20** Apron

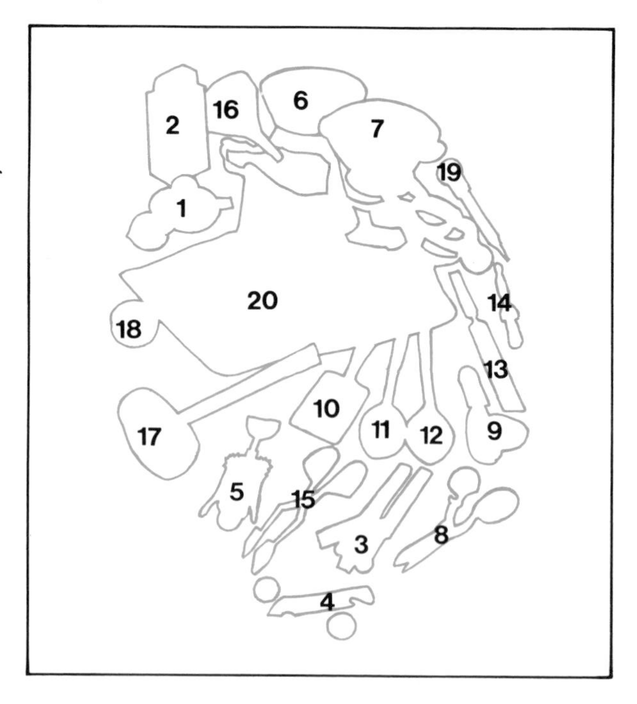

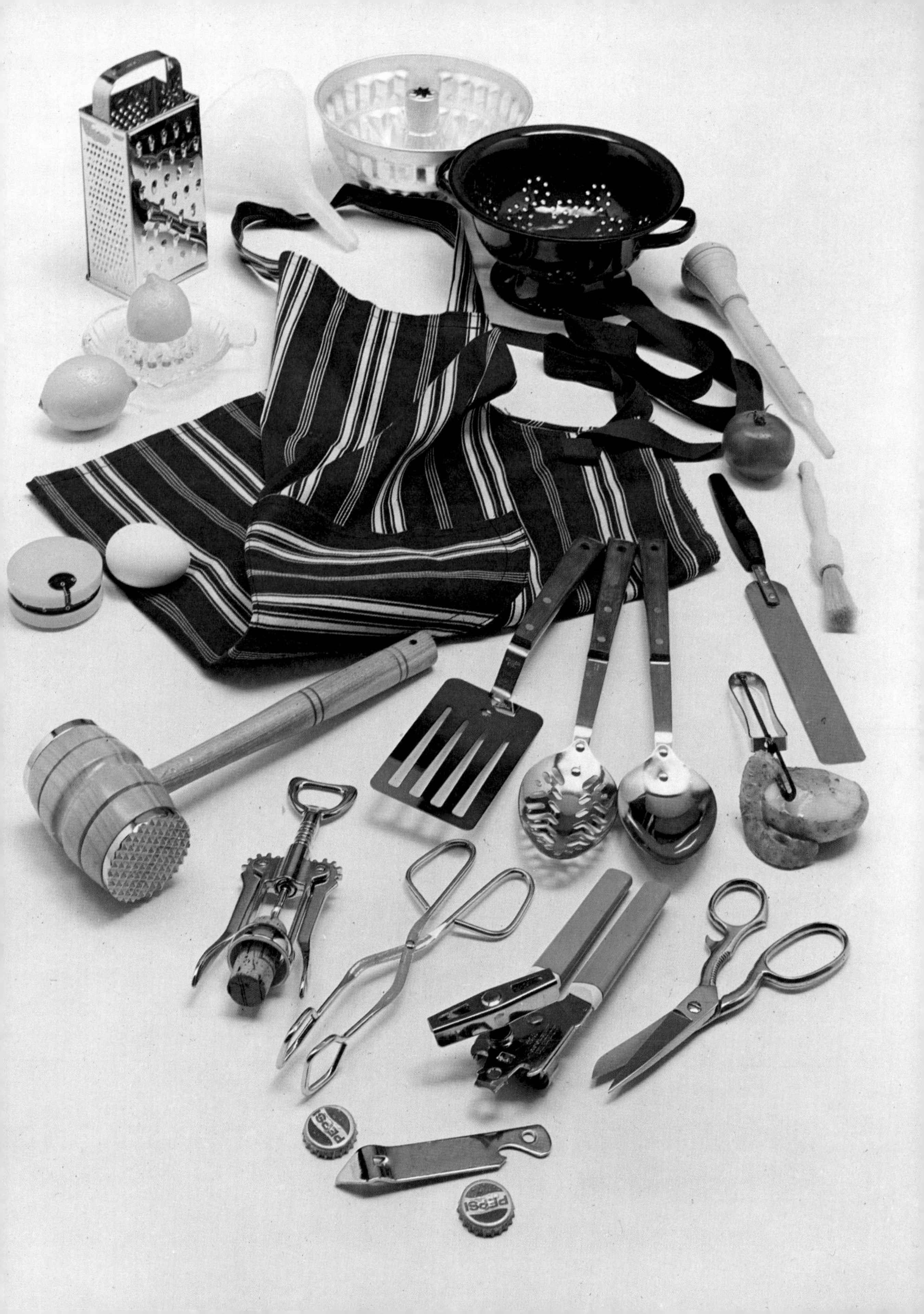
PEPSI
PEPSI

# Nice but not Essential

Once you have the basic equipment you need, there are other kitchen tools you'd probably like to have. You won't be accused of just collecting gadgets if you choose from among the utensils shown here. They're not essential, it's true, but they are handy and helpful.

**1** Deep fat fryer with basket
**2** Omelet pan
**3** Egg poacher
**4** Meat thermometer
**5** Oven thermometer
**6** Soufflé dishes
**7** Flan rings
**8** Assorted cookie cutters
**9** Pestle and mortar
**10** Chicken scissors
**11** Icing bag set
**12** Cheese grater
**13** Egg slicer
**14** Jar opener
**15** Food mill
**16** Trussing needle and thread
**17** Ricer
**18** Custard cups

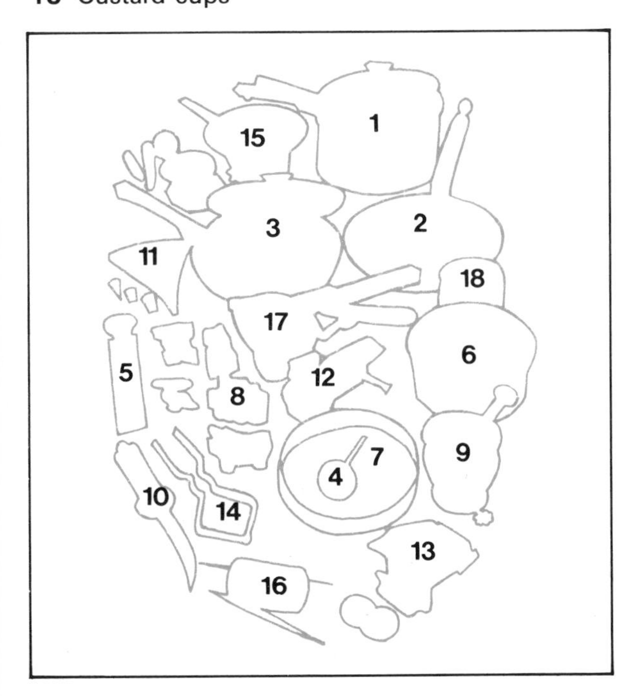


attachments of your mixer can do the job in minutes. The grinder is invaluable if you like to make meat loaf. It takes just seconds to fix fruit desserts, purées, and ice cream sauces in the blender. You can also make delicious soups, and fruit and vegetable cocktails in this useful attachment. If you want to try freezing and canning, you can rely on your mixer to take away a lot of the hard work in preparing fruits and vegetables. As for baking—well that's what the mixer was first all about, wasn't it?

Perhaps you don't do a great amount of cooking, but like to have some extra help when you're preparing a special meal. For you, a hand mixer and a separate blender will probably do perfectly. The hand mixer can beat up a cake mix as well as a heavy duty mixer, whip egg whites and cream, and stir light cake batters or pancakes you make from scratch. You can use the blender for soups, sauces, sandwich fillings, fruit and vegetable purées, instant desserts, and baby foods. It will also make breadcrumbs, chop fresh herbs, and grind coffee beans. These two smaller pieces of equipment, in fact, can accomplish

Below: a pressure cooker saves a lot of time in making stock, stews, and other long, slow dishes. Many a cook wouldn't want to be without one.

# Electric Appliances

Few modern homes are without at least one or two of the electric appliances that save so much effort and time in cooking. In fact, there are whole books devoted just to blender cooking, or electric frying pan cookery. The equipment shown here is among the most popular—and the most basic—for your kitchen use.

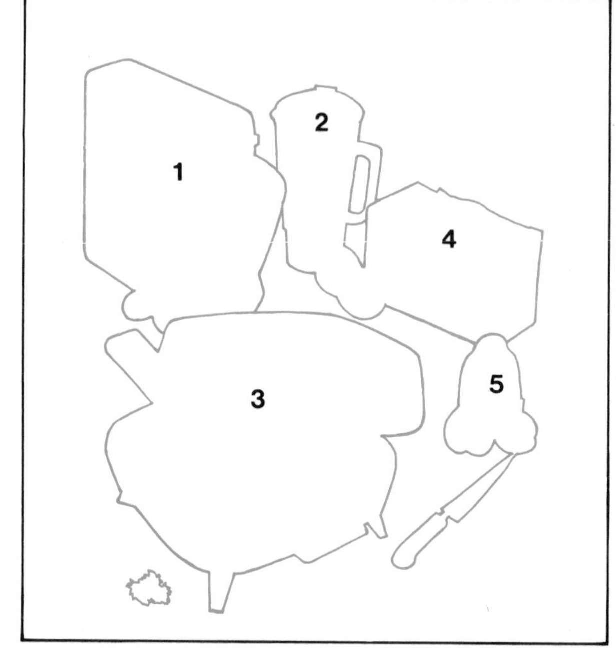


**1** Mixer
**2** Blender
**3** Frying Pan
**4** Toaster
**5** Knife Sharpener

most cooking preparations in a small household, and are far more economical than a full-size all-purpose mixer.

It could be that you are one of the many prospective brides or wives who have been given a mixer as a present. So, you're the proud owner of a luxury piece of equipment without having decided you want it, or what you can do with it. Often husbands buy their wives a blender with the secret idea that it will be fun to use for making cocktails; but it would be a pity if it were only used then. When you're given any kind of kitchen equipment, read the instruction booklet from cover to cover to find out exactly what the machine can do for you. If necessary, ask a demonstrator to come and demonstrate it in your own home, or call and see her at your local department store. If a demonstrator isn't on hand, don't hesitate to write to the manufacturer for further information, recipe ideas, and other advice you would like to have about your newly acquired equipment. Make it into a useful aid rather than a dust-collecting gadget.

When you have the right equipment, you are all set to tackle amost any recipe that takes your fancy. A well organized kitchen also helps you work efficiently, and reduces fatigue. Some cooks seem to like to work in a muddle —or what they might prefer to call "organized chaos". Generally speaking, however, systematic planning of work in a well-arranged and equipped kitchen is the recipe for successful cooking. When there is a place for everything—enough working surfaces to avoid clutter, plenty of shelves, racks, drawers, and cupboards, and equipment just where it is needed—the kitchen is a delightful place to work in. No one wants to go on a forced

KENWOOD chef

Left: your ideal kitchen may be one that looks and is ultra-modern. Above: the special touch in this efficient kitchen is the fold-away table that turns into desk or work space.

march from range to sink to drain the vegetables, or to a drawer to find a wire whisk while the sauce threatens to lump.

**Guidelines for an efficient kitchen**

Here are some suggestions that will save steps and help you improve your skills in the kitchen. For example, it is useful to have working surfaces on either side of your range, and also on either side of your sink unit. This way you can control the flow to and from the particular appliance. If your range and sink are next to each other, separate them by one working surface. Then you can put used pots and pans from the stove on it, ready to go into the sink to soak, and put vegetables and similar foods prepared at the sink on it, ready to go onto the range to cook.

Your refrigerator and general storage cupboard should be close to your main working surface. Beneath it should be cupboards to hold pans, bowls, measuring cups, baking pans, and so on. The top of this working surface is the place to keep your mixer out, plugged in, and ready for action.

You may be surprised at the idea, but food storage cupboards with narrow shelves are best—10 to 12 inches in width is ideal. Wider than this, and items at the back get lost—or, just as bad, the back of the cupboard becomes filled with almost empty containers you really should be using up. If you're stuck with deep shelves, try putting a row of empty boxes (sturdy ones) along the back. When you place cans and packets on this raised surface you'll be able to see them above what's in front.

Keep small tools, and plenty of them, just where they will be needed. A wide jug with

Above: one of the handiest arrangements for your spices is a cupboard that has additional shelves in the door. Having it just next to the range is as convenient as could be.
Left: holders that look like plastic baskets, and that slide in and out like file drawers, solve the problem of vegetable storage simply, easily, and attractively. It could be your solution, too.

wooden spoons, whisks, spatulas, and scrapers by the range, and another by the main working surface speed your work—and look nice, too, with their contrasting shapes and materials.

People often think their kitchens are too small, but seldom consider that a big kitchen might be inefficient. If you have room for all standing and stored equipment and foodstuff, plus room to move about easily, your kitchen is probably the right size. If you have to walk more than three or four steps between range, refrigerator, sink, and working surfaces, the kitchen could be too big.

Of course, a big room allows space for use as a "kitchen office" or dining area if the work area is set off by an island divider. Then you might happily have the ideal kitchen. Just think of the pleasure of having an area free

from splashes, spills, and the heat of cooking, where you can sit to read recipes, make or check shopping lists, browse through cookbooks, and even do some of the household bookkeeping. This is also the perfect spot for a phone extension and a bulletin board. Make your bulletin board decorative as well as useful by tacking up the children's latest artistic masterpieces and a few of your favorite postcards, photos, or prints. On the practical side, keep lists of things to buy daily or weekly on the bulletin board, post your menu plan on it, and keep your dinner party timetable of things to do and buy on it.

What layout should the ideal kitchen have? The square U-shape is usually considered best, although a long narrow one is also known to be efficient. Either shape can be partly achieved by an island unit in the right place.

Unless you're planning a new kitchen from scratch, it is not usually convenient to make great changes. However, you can often rearrange one or two movable units to make the kitchen more convenient. For example, what about moving a floor cupboard with a work top between the range and sink? Can you reposition the refrigerator nearer the main preparation area? Try putting up small wall units and shelves to hold essential supplies and equipment exactly where they are most needed. A magnetic knife rack can be hung in a little wall space—it will hold your sharp knives ready for use, and safely away from vulnerable fingers plunged all unsuspecting into a drawer. Wall mounted spice and storage jars can hold seasonings and basic ingredients where they are wanted.

You'll also want to keep your cookbooks where the action is to get the best use of them.

If your kitchen is big enough, it's great to have an office corner. Left: you can keep your recipe file up to date while still keeping an eye on the saucepan.

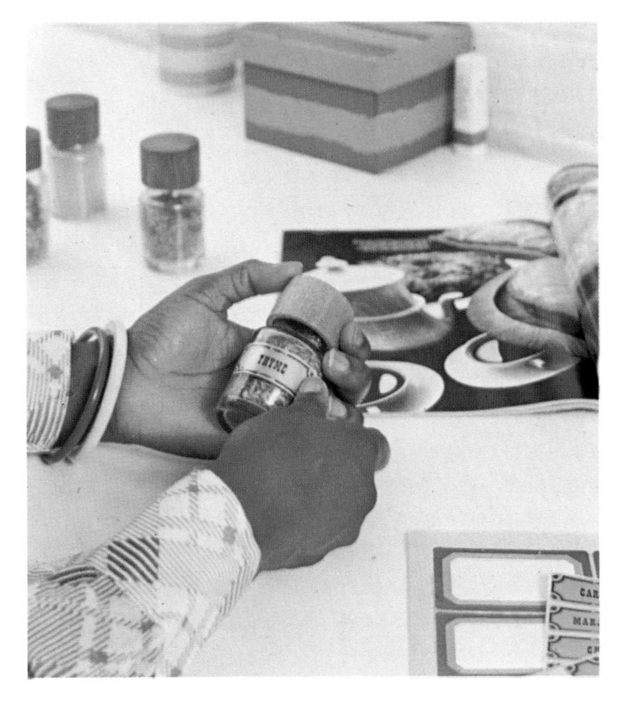

Right: filling your own spice jars saves money. Use your office nook to label the jars prettily.

Cookbooks need to be handy when you're trying out a brand new recipe, or when you have to refer to a favorite recipe often, or check up on a new serving method. Some of us like to read cookbooks for the fun of it—and some cookbooks make good reading. Like equipment, however, the cookbooks you buy for yourself are a highly personal choice. Some cooks like to have rows of cookbooks, while others have only two or three favorites. The actual number doesn't determine how good a cook you are, as we all know.

You may even be tempted to say that cookbooks are only for beginners; but, at the same time, if you think of the best cooks you know, you'll probably realize how often they read and consult cookbooks. This is because the more you cook, and the more experienced you become, the more urgent is the need for new recipes. The art of cooking is partly dependent on a fund of bright new recipes—from cookbooks, magazines, newspapers, and friends. The art of cooking is also dependent on interesting and new twists on well-loved and well-known recipes, perhaps those treasured hand-me-downs from mother and grandmother. It is the individuality you bring to basic recipes, and the new zing you put into tried-and-true ones that make you a cook worthy to be called an artist.

Helping you work from important basic recipes with imagination and inspiration comes in a later chapter, as do hints on how to save a dish when something goes wrong. Your interest, your sense of adventure, and your effort—added to skills and approaches you can learn from these pages—are your foundations for the art of cooking.

# What Happens When You Cook 2

Have you ever wondered about what actually happens to food when you prepare it for eating? You know, for example, that meat shrinks when cooked, and that egg added to sauce thickens the mixture. You also know that fish cooks more quickly than meat, and that vegetables soften by being cooked. Why? The explanations come from science, for cooking is a science as well as an art. For instance, think of the chemical leavening agent in baking powder. It works to produce the gases that make feather light sponge and chiffon cakes. Many of the color changes between raw and cooked foods are the result of chemical changes. Even loss of nutritive value during cooking is the result of a chain of chemical reactions. Of course, we don't want to take cookery out of the kitchen and into the laboratory. However, we think it will help you get the best out of food if you know something about its composition, the changes that can take place within it, and what is likely to be happening inside the bowl, the pan, or the oven.

Let's take a look at a piece of meat with the eye of the expert. You'll see that a roasting or broiling cut is fine textured, and has a velvety look. It doesn't have any obvious pieces of gristle, it is covered with a firm outer covering of fat, and it is evenly flecked inside with tiny pieces of fat called marbling. Looking at cuts suitable for braising and stewing, you see that the meat is much coarser in texture. It has little marbling, and may have some gristle—in sheets or as tendons or ligaments. Judge for freshness by smell and feel, if the meat is not packaged. Fresh meat should have a not unpleasant smell, and should not feel slimy or sticky.

Toughness of meat depends on the age of the animal, and the part of the body from which the meat was cut. The older the animal, the tougher its flesh. One guide to age is the color of the fat in the meat. For example, beef fat from a young animal will usually be creamy white, and that from an older animal will likely be much more yellow. Remember, though, that this is not an infallible guide, because an animal's diet also affects the color of its fat.

The trend these days is to assure tenderness in meat by using comparatively young animals. Pigs are usually slaughtered at six to seven months of age, for example; steers just before they are one-year-old; and lambs at between four and six months of age. Mutton is almost a meat of the past today, when tenderness is of prime importance to the majority of people. Although an older animal's meat develops more flavor, it is too tough for many tastes.

Where do the tough and tender cuts come from? Well-used muscles, such as those in the leg, are much tougher than muscles that do little work, such as those beneath the backbone. (From here comes the highly prized tenderloin.) However, the more the muscle is used, the more flavorful it is likely to be. That is why some people prefer the slightly tougher, but richer flavored sirloin steak to the extremely tender, but flatter tasting filet mignon. As for poultry, battery-reared chickens, whose physical movements

As you handle the raw materials of the family dinner, have you ever wondered about what cooking really does to them to make them eatable? Knowing something about the science of cooking can be useful—and fun.

Tho Pinfold
Banbury

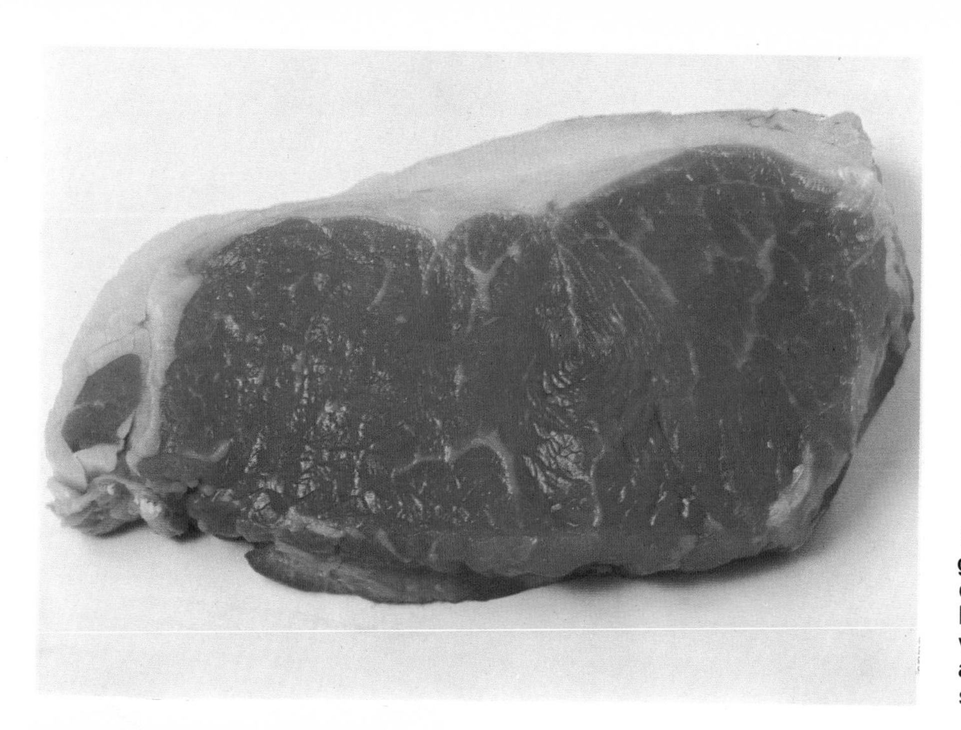

Left and below left: here you can see the difference between tender meat that can be broiled, and tough meat that must be stewed. The steak at the top is lean but well marbled; the meat below is full of gristle.

Right: this handy chart gives you a quick reference to which cuts of beef to use for various ways of preparation, and which part of the steer they come from.

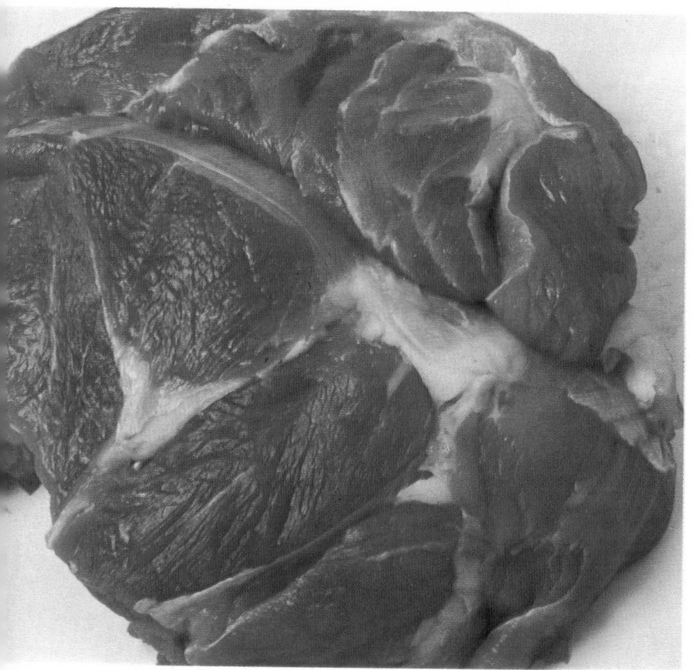

are restricted, are never as flavorful as farmyard free-range birds, allowed to roam at will.

Fortunately, even the toughest meat can be tenderized with proper and careful cooking. Think of the good old-fashioned boiling chicken, gently simmered for hours to a melt-in-the-mouth tenderness without loss of mouthwatering flavor. On the other hand, think how much careful seasoning has to be done to improve the mild flavor of the extremely tender broiling chicken, even though the cooking time is short.

As muscles become better developed and efficient with maturity, they become stronger and more tightly bound with a material known to scientists as "connective tissue", and to cooks as gristle. There are two kinds of connective tissue: the white, which binds muscle fibers together, and the yellow, which is in the form of ligaments and tendons joining muscle to bone. Muscles that are not used vigorously have far less connective tissue than hard-working muscles. Therefore, meat with more connective tissue is tougher. During long slow cooking in a moist atmosphere—by braising, pot roasting, boiling, or stewing—white connective tissue is converted into gelatine, and the tough meat softens. Yellow connective tissue is unaffected by any cooking method, but can easily be cut out.

Another constituent that affects tenderness of meat is its fat, both the outside layer and the flecks of marbling between the lean muscle fibers. Although fat meat is not popular, meat that is too lean will be tough. The tenderizing effect of fat is thought to result from the way the fat melts and seeps out of the meat during cooking, so exposing

# Know Your Beef Cuts

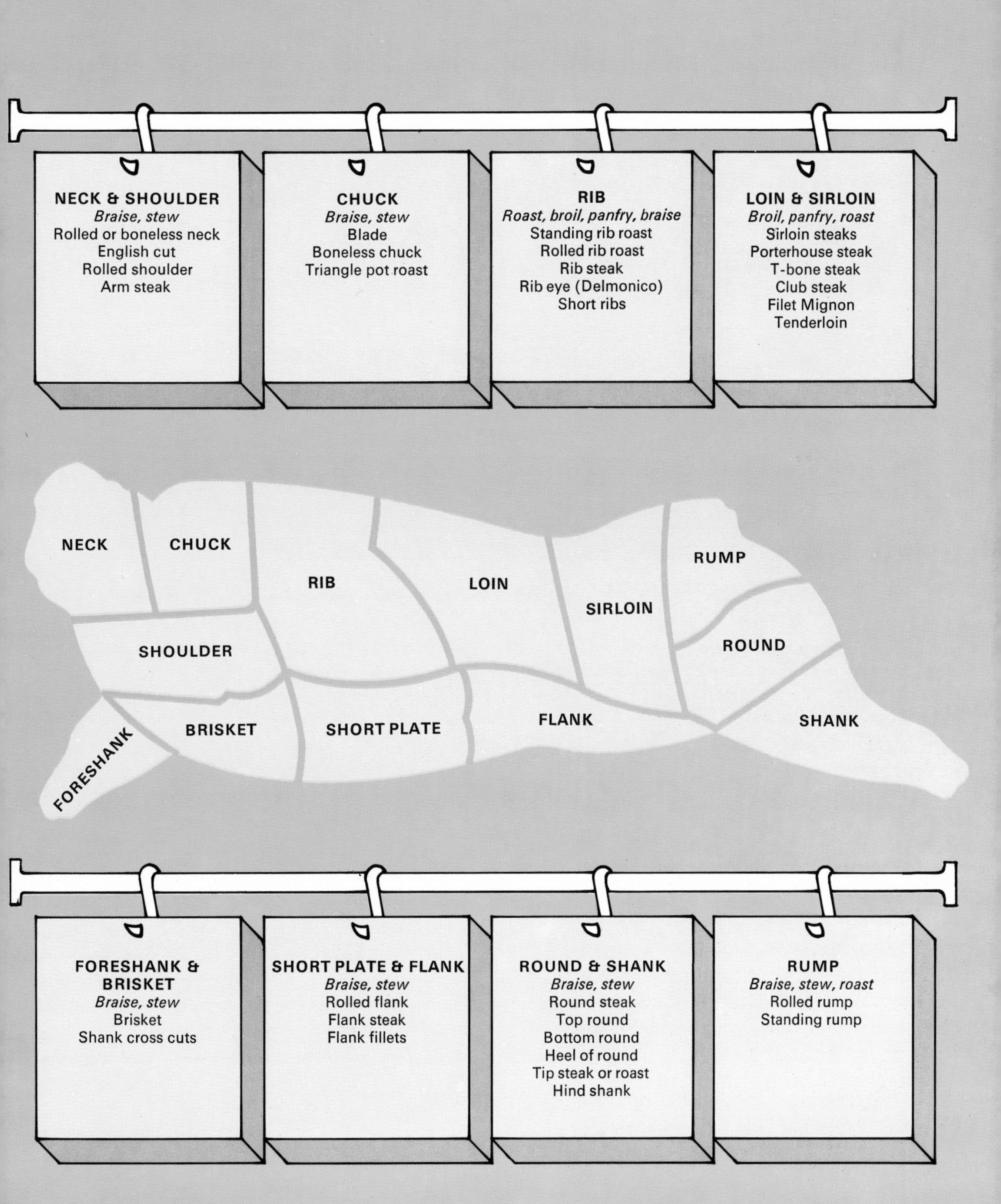

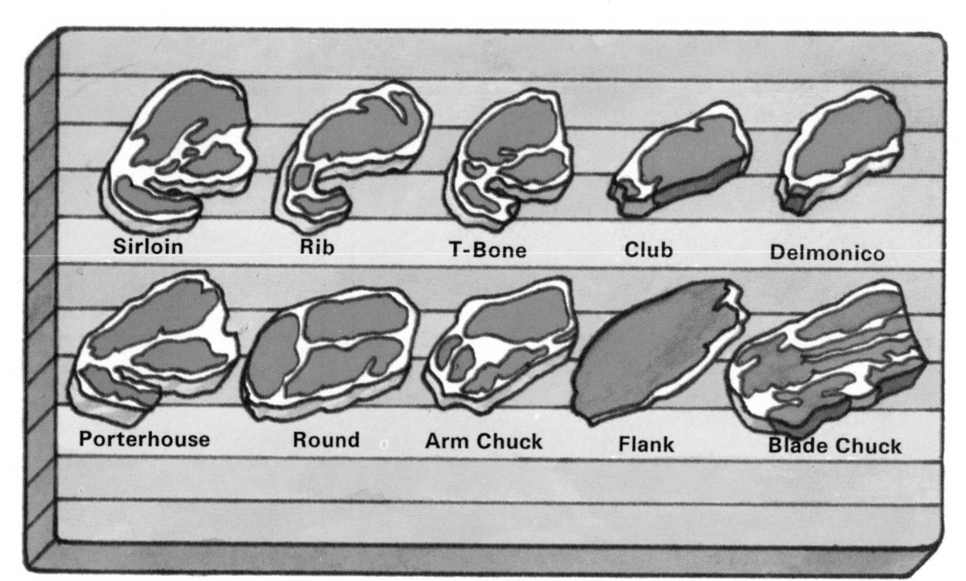


Left: beef is the all-American favorite, and steak ranks highest of the beef cuts. The first six steaks shown here are the tender broiling cuts; the others usually must be braised, unless they are prime quality.

Right: use this chart as a guide to which pork cuts are suitable for which way of preparation.

the connective tissue to softening by heat. A high fat content in meat makes it self-tenderizing. That is the reason why all cuts of pork can be roasted or broiled, while only some cuts of beef and lamb are suitable for these cooking methods.

Roasts with a thin outer layer of fat are tougher than those with a more generous outer covering of fat. Such a roast, which is cheaper in cost, can be improved by covering it with extra fat, or by basting it frequently. A lower oven temperature, and correspondingly longer cooking time, can also tenderize a roast having little outside fat. Poultry and most variety meats, including liver, have low natural fat content. Basting takes care of keeping roast chicken or turkey from drying out, and slow braising is the best for keeping variety meats both tender and juicy.

What happens to meat in the cooking process? When meat is subjected to any kind of heat, the proteins within the muscle fibers begin to contract. As they do, they squeeze out the meat juices within the fibers. The fiercer the heat, or the longer the overall cooking period, the more the fibers shrink, and the harder the meat becomes. This is not a contradiction to the rule that tough meat will get tender with long, slow cooking. It will get tough and hard *again* if it is overcooked.

Some cooks like to start roasts in a hot oven—400°F or even more—for the first 15 or 20 minutes, and then reduce the oven temperature to 325° or 350°F for the rest of the cooking time. The initial high temperature seals the outside of the meat, and helps to reduce moisture loss from the inside. (For the same reason, steaks should always be put under a red hot broiler, or on a fiery hot barbecue. If you prefer, you can sear the outside of your steaks in sizzling hot oil or butter in a heavy skillet before broiling or barbecuing.) The crisp outer coating of a

# Know Your Pork Cuts

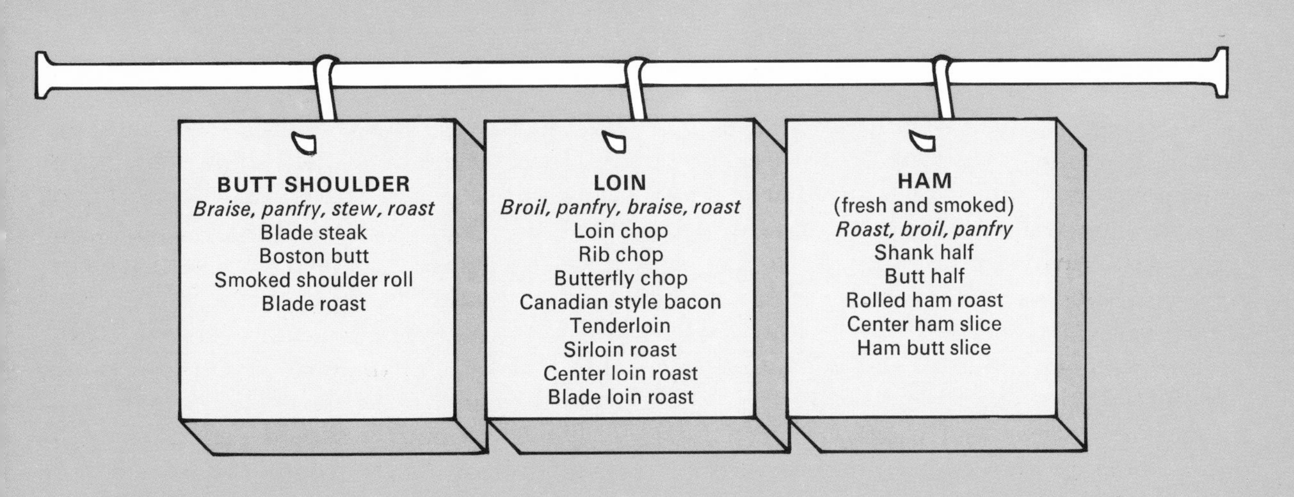


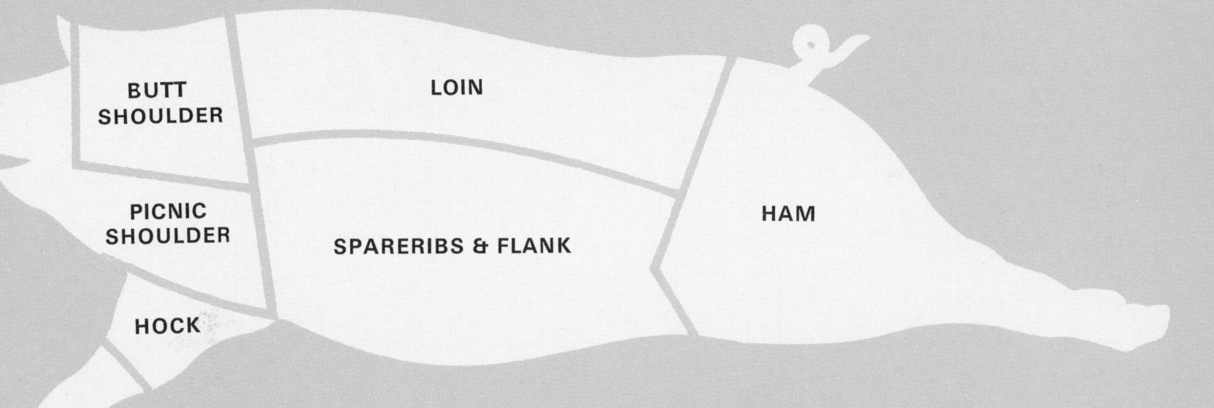


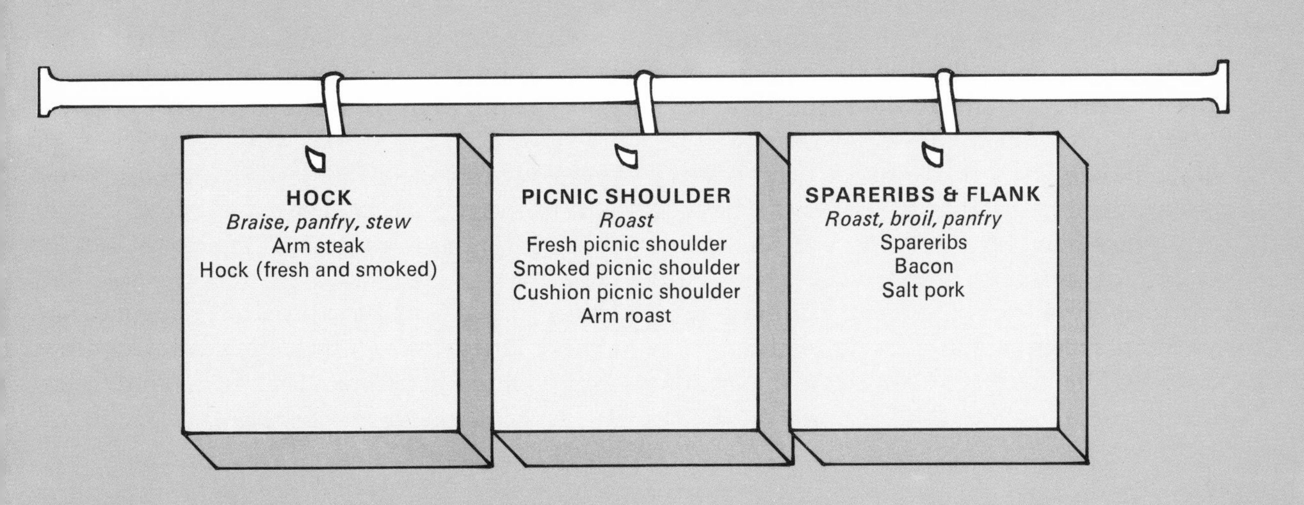

Right: if you want to try other lamb cuts besides the popular chops or leg, get some idea of how to cook them for best results from this chart.

seared roast or steak is most attractive, but the high-temperature cooking must be carefully controlled unless you want your meat to be extremely well done through and through. An overcooked roast becomes dry and tasteless because all its flavor-carrying juices drain into the roasting pan. The juices make a flavorful gravy, but this cannot compensate for the flavorless, overdone roast.

Although stews and casseroles need long slow cooking, they can also be overdone. Overcooked stewing meat becomes dry, stringy, and tough. With overcooking, the meat fibers have squeezed out all the natural juices of the meat. The cooking liquid will then have a wonderful flavor, but the meat practically none at all. Of course, when making stocks or soups, we deliberately overcook the meat so that all its flavor is transferred to the liquid in which it is being cooked. If a stew or stock sets to a jelly on cooling, you know that the long, moist cooking has converted to gelatine all the gristle originally in the meat.

Another chemical reaction in the cooking of meat changes its color from red or pink to brown. This color change is brought about by the effect of heat on the meat pigments. It is convenient for us cooks that the change from pink to brown occurs at the same time that we would consider the meat to be done. This color change is a good guide to the correct cooking time for roasts if you don't have a meat thermometer. Simply run a sharp skewer, or a sharp pronged fork, into the center of the meat, and gently squeeze out some of the meat juices. The meat is adquately cooked if the juices are colorless. If you like your meat rare, take it out of the oven when the juices are still of a slightly pink color.

Meat thermometers take some of the guesswork out of timing roasts. Let the meat cook until the thermometer registers slightly *less* than the degree to which you want it done. This is because the inside of the meat retains the heat, and will continue to cook to the right degree after the meat has been removed from the oven.

The thermometer should penetrate to the center of the meat. Estimate how deep you should put it in by measuring the thermometer shaft against the side of the roast first of all. Then make a hole to the center of the meat with a skewer. When inserting the thermometer, make sure the pointed end does not rest on fat or bone.

Always keep the meat in the oven when you read the thermometer, and check the reading often and carefully as the meat approaches the end of cooking. The temperature increases rapidly at this stage.

Now, let's match some specific meat cuts to the way they should be prepared for most tenderness and taste. Cheap, tough cuts need the long slow cooking of stewing or braising. In beef, such cuts include heel of round, shank, plate, flank, and neck. The neck, shank, and breast of lamb fall into this category. Tender cuts of meat, with little connective tissue, can be cooked quickly at the high temperatures used in roasting, broiling, and panbroiling. Such beef cuts include rib, short loin, sirloin, and all steaks. Among the tender cuts are the leg, shoulder, and rib and loin chops. Veal cuts for this preparation include blade, rib, loin, and sirloin. Remember that cooking is not required to tenderize the meat. In fact, the tender cuts of meat are

# Know Your Lamb Cuts

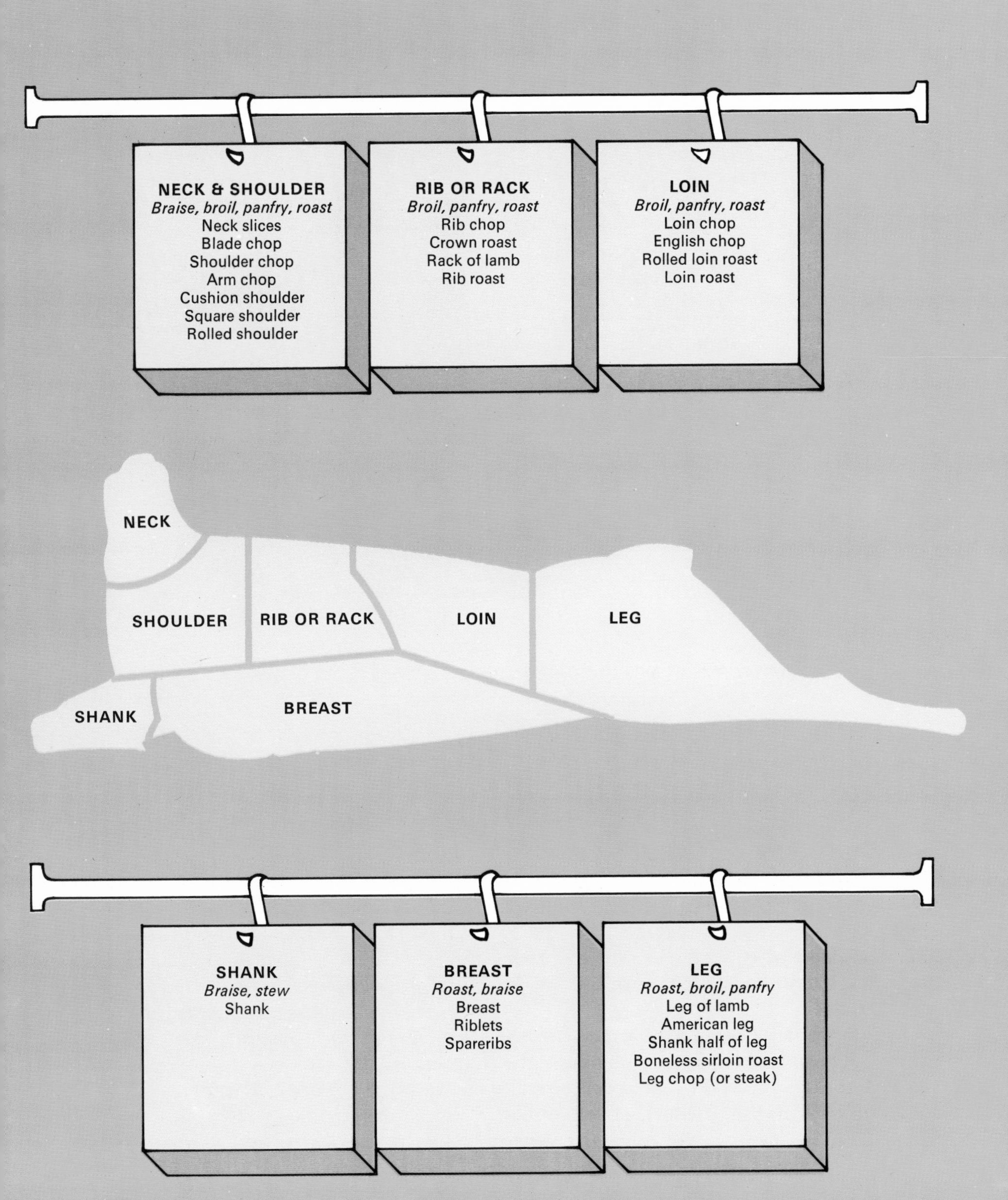

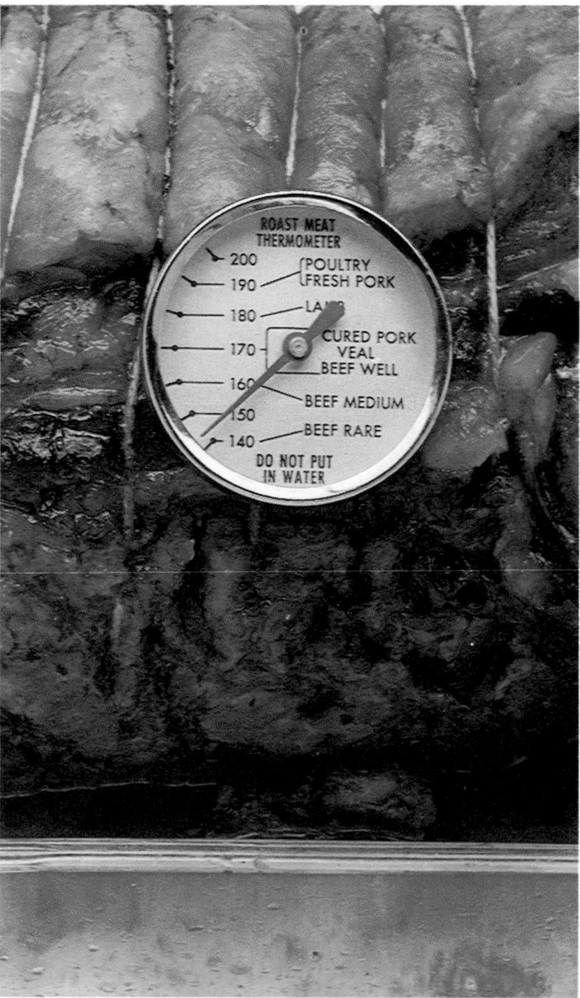

Right and below: a meat thermometer takes a lot of the guesswork out of deciding when a roast is done. Put the thermometer in the thickest part of the meat without touching bone. Take the roast out just before the needle is on the indication line you want.

best cooked rare, or slightly underdone, to preserve their flavor and maximum juiciness. Pork, of course, is the exception; it should always be thoroughly cooked through to the center of the meat.

Cuts that are fairly tender but still have a moderate amount of connective tissue, any meat from an older animal, or any meat you are in two minds about, are best cooked by braising or pot roasting. In these methods, the meat is cooked in a small amount of liquid that is not enough to cover the meat, but enough to provide a moist atmosphere for slow cooking.

So far, we have been concerned with the science of meat cookery. Let's look next at fish.

With meat, you choose a method to suit its tenderness. With fish, the method you choose depends more on its flavor and fat content, because all fish is tender. The muscle fibers of fish are shorter, they contain much less connective tissue than meat, and have none of the type of connective tissue that never dissolves.

Fish vary in their texture, with some being coarser than others. The finer the texture, the finer the flavor is a maxim that usually holds true. Fish also vary in the amount of oil in their flesh. White fish, such as sole, cod, flounder, ocean perch, and haddock, contain very little fat, while salmon, shad, swordfish, and tuna have a fat content similar to that of meat. Shellfish is also low in fat. Generally speaking, lean white fish has a milder flavor than oily fish.

Because of the small amount of connective tissue, fish tends to flake and break easily when it is cooked, and it is all too easy to overcook fish. Cooking times are always shorter than for an equal weight of meat. During cooking, protein in the fish muscle fibers contract like those in meat fibers. Overcooked fish not only breaks up, but also becomes dry, and loses flavor.

The aim in cooking top quality fish, such as salmon, sole, and halibut is to preserve its fine flavor. The best way to do this is to poach such fish, in a fish stock made from selected herbs and fish trimmings, or in white wine with a small bouquet of herbs.

On the other hand, coarse white fish, such as cod and haddock, are improved if you add flavor to them during cooking. You can do this by stuffing them, or by using herbs and spices. You can also add the flavor afterward by serving with a well-flavored sauce. Another way to do coarse lean fish is to first poach it in milk in the oven or on the top of the range. Then use the cooking liquid as the basis of a sauce to which you add cheese, chopped hardboiled egg, or other seasonings.

If you want to cook a large fish whole, you should really use a fish kettle. However, you can cook whole fish wrapped in a generous envelope of foil in the oven. To oven-bake whole fish like this, carefully dry the fish and then brush with melted butter. Add slices of lemon and a few fresh herbs if you have them —dill, fennel, parsley, marjoram, or chervil are good choices. Wrap the fish and seasonings in a large piece of foil, so that the fish cooks in the butter and its own juices.

Most fish can be easily broiled whole, or as

Below: for a test without a thermometer, prick the roast. If the juices run red, it is rare; pink, medium; colorless, well done.

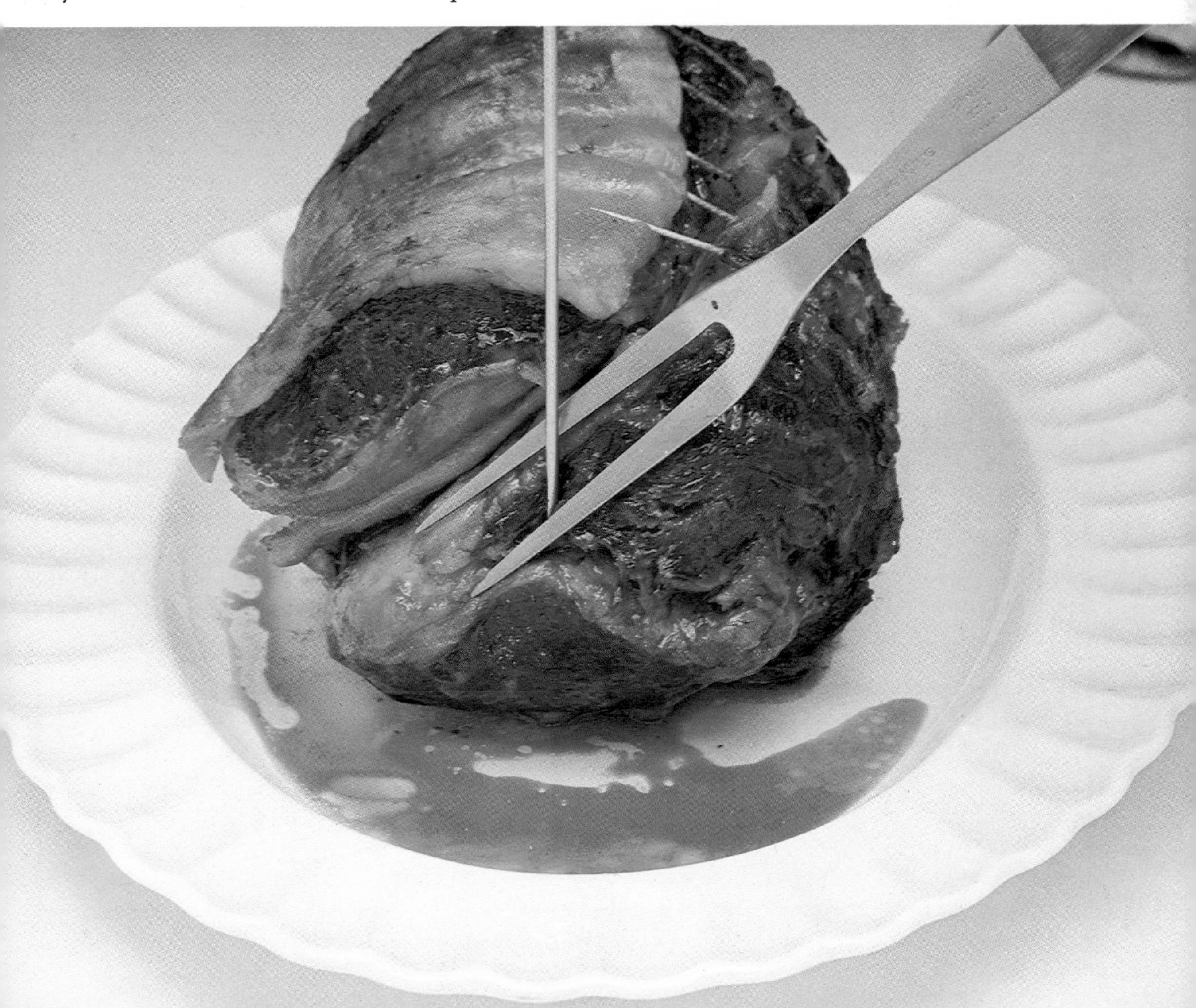

Left: fish baked in foil with lemon and herbs comes out beautifully juicy and tasty.

Right: this chart tells you at a glance how to best cook the most common of our fish.

steaks or fillets. A simple basting sauce of butter, salt, freshly ground pepper, and a squeeze of lemon is all that is required for delicious flavor. You can barbecue in a similar way to broiling, or wrapped in foil as for baking. Fatty fish can be broiled or barbecued especially well. You don't need to baste them at all, but gently cook them in their own oil.

In choosing fish for frying, remember that fat or oily fish are too rich to be deep fried, but are perfect for panbroiling. Their flesh usually supplies enough oil to prevent sticking, but you may want to lightly grease the skillet with cooking oil to make sure. Coarse white fish is the most suitable for deep frying.

When you fry fish, you must coat it to stop it from absorbing too much fat, and also to prevent it from breaking up. The ideal coating is one that cooks quickly and firmly, not only to do the two jobs already mentioned, but also to provide an attractive, crisp outside. Try seasoned breadcrumbs, or well crushed cornflakes or cracker crumbs as a coating. Crushed potato chips give an unusual coating for small pieces of fish. A batter coating is best for deep frying. You can make your own or use a pancake mix. In either case, a dash of dried herbs or spices, such as paprika, barbecue seasoning, or curry powder, gives extra flavor to the batter.

For panfrying fish, use either clarified butter or your usual cooking oil. For deep frying, cooking oil is ideal. If you plan to reuse the oil, strain it well to get rid of the tiny pieces of

Below: you fillet small or large fish somewhat differently. To fillet a small one, place it on its side with the backbone toward you, as on left of diagram. Starting below the fin near the tail, cut toward the head along the backbone, using a sliding motion toward and along the rib bones until the fillet is freed. Do it all in one piece, as shown by the dash lines on left drawing. To fillet a large fish, split it from vent to tail. Begin at the tail, and separate the flesh from the backbone, loosening it also from the rib bones. You will get a double fillet as illustrated on the right.

# Cooking Fish

| | Broil | Fry | Deep Fry | Steam | Bake | Poach |
|---|---|---|---|---|---|---|
| Cod | ■ | ■ | ■ | ■ | ■ | ■ |
| Haddock | ■ | ■ | ■ | | ■ | ■ |
| Mackerel | ■ | | | | | |
| Whitefish | ■ | | ■ | | | |
| Trout | ■ | ■ | | | | ■ |
| Sole | ■ | ■ | ■ | | | ■ |
| Flounder | ■ | ■ | ■ | ■ | | |
| Whiting | ■ | | ■ | | | |
| Salmon | ■ | | | ■ | ■ | ■ |
| Tuna | ■ | | | | | |
| Halibut | ■ | | | | | ■ |
| Swordfish | ■ | | | | | |
| Perch | | ■ | ■ | | | |
| Rockfish | | ■ | | | | |
| Butterfish | | ■ | ■ | | | |
| Sunfish | | ■ | | | | |
| Bream | | ■ | | | | |
| Porgy | | ■ | ■ | | | |
| Mullet | | ■ | | | | |
| Smelts | ■ | ■ | ■ | | | |
| Bluefish | ■ | | | ■ | ■ | |
| Bass | | | | ■ | ■ | |
| Scrod | ■ | | | ■ | | |
| Red Snapper | | | | ■ | ■ | ■ |
| Carp | | | | ■ | | ■ |
| Shad | | | | | ■ | |

coating that become detached during cooking. If you deep fry fish regularly, you'll find it a good idea to keep a supply of oil solely for cooking fish.

Before serving, drain fried and deep fried fish on paper towels. If you don't, the fish will not only be rather greasy, but its coating will lose its crispness. Don't keep fried fish warm in a covered dish. It is best placed on a warm, uncovered dish in a warm but unlit oven. Ideally, fried fish should be taken out of the pan, quickly but efficiently drained, and served immediately.

To offset the fattiness of fried fish you should serve a slightly acid sauce—tartare or other mayonnaise or sour cream based ones, piquant lemon sauce, or horseradish sauce.

Although New England and New York vie in fame for their clam chowders, most Americans don't think of fish for soup. Yet all coarse lean fish and shellfish are ideal for chowders and soups. The famous Mediterranean fish dish known as "bouillabaisse" originated as a simple fisherman's soup, made from the day's catch, or the unsaleable bits and pieces left at the end of the day. It is usually made with a number of different kinds of fish—the more the variety, the better the flavor. Care should be taken not to over-

Here are two tests for freshness of eggs. Left: a fresh egg broken onto a plate will have a yolk that stays up in a dome, and whites that are thick and translucent, as on the right. A stale egg's yolk goes flat, and the white is runny, as on the left.

Below left: placed in a bowl of cold water, a fresh egg will sink to the bottom, as in the top photo. An old egg will stay afloat.

cook fish even in soups. If you do, you'll end up with tough tasteless flakes floating on top of the liquid.

How often have you used the expression, "She can't even cook an egg?" In fact, this saying is not usually apt, because it is not easy to cook eggs properly. (Think of those rubbery fried eggs, those greenish yolks in hardboiled eggs, those curdled sauces.) Understanding the science of egg cookery a little ought to help overcome some of the pitfalls.

Eggs are unique in being one of nature's own prepackaged convenience foods. Nutritionally they are the most complete of all foods, and the food value of many other foods are compared with a hen's egg. They are also very versatile, and can be cooked in an amazing number of different ways. All these factors make it even more important to master the art of cooking them just right.

It's mainly a question of judging the right cooking temperature. With eggs, the rule always is gentle heat. Like all proteins contained in food, egg proteins begin to contract, and gradually become more and more solid as they are heated. When you first drop an egg into boiling water, the white part becomes translucent, and then opaque as the egg white proteins solidify. If you boil an egg instead of gently simmering it, the white becomes very tough, and loses some of its flavor, even though the egg could not be described as being overcooked. If you do hardboil an egg in bubbling, boiling water, the white hardens to a leatherlike texture, and the hard yolk becomes coated with a stubborn greenish black stain.

When you scramble eggs, you should always use gentle heat. If the butter is already sizzling in a very hot pan when you add the eggs, they may well shrivel up—and your scrambled eggs will be a mixture of tough rubbery pieces floating in a colorless liquid. If you scramble eggs over low heat, the egg proteins will only gradually thicken, and so stay fairly soft and creamy.

As you know, eggs are often used to thicken sauces or soups. This is because as the egg

Right: it's not very appetizing to find a heavy greenish stain on the yolk of a hardboiled egg. You can avoid this by gently simmering, rather than briskly boiling eggs.

Left: overcooking cheese will make a sauce lumpy and dry. What you can't see is that overcooked cheese is also indigestible.

Right: cheese fondue as the Swiss do it is an attractive, flavorsome, and satisfying main dish. The diners all dip their own bread cubes into the cheese themselves, so it's an easy dish to do for a party, too.

proteins begin to solidify, they enmesh the other liquids present so that the whole mixture appears to thicken. If you heat such a mixture at too high a temperature, the egg proteins coagulate too quickly, and do not have the chance to enmesh the other liquids. What then happens is that the egg proteins set to tough leathery strands, leaving the watery fluid around them. This is the state we usually describe as "curdling", the curds being the coagulated proteins.

When thickening a sauce or a soup with eggs, a double boiler is a safeguard against curdling. This works because the water under the mixture prevents the temperature in the top pan from getting too high. Remember also to take extreme care when reheating a mixture containing eggs—a creamed soup, or fish or poultry in a rich sauce, for example. They should be reheated slowly, stirred regularly, and attended every minute. If in any doubt, stand the dish in a larger dish or pan containing boiling water, and put in the oven.

Oven temperatures are critical to proper cooking of baked egg dishes, such as soufflé, custard, and shirred eggs. An oven thermometer is a great help in making sure the oven heat is right.

Proteins in egg white set at a slightly lower temperature than yolk proteins. This explains why there is such a thing as a softboiled egg, which has a fairly solid white with a runny yolk. Because the yolk proteins begin to thicken at a slightly higher temperature, yolks alone are often used to thicken sauces and soups. In this case, the mixture can be heated at somewhat higher heat, and the danger of curdling is delayed.

Egg whites come into their own with regard to beating. Both whites and yolks will beat to a fairly stable foam, but whites alone produce a much greater volume. That is why we usually separate the yolks and whites when making very light, fluffy dishes such as soufflés and mousses. The yolks are beaten into the mixture for richness, and the stiffly beaten whites are folded in at the end.

Some people think of cheese only as a snack food, but it is more versatile than that. Just think of the ways you can cook with cheese—cheese pies and soufflés, cheese sauces, toasted cheese, cheese pastries, cheese dips, main dish fondues. Cheese puts a bite into the crisp gratin topping on vegetables and other dishes; finely chopped grated cheese is delicious floating on top of piping hot soup—and almost everyone's mouth waters at the thought of a yummy piece of cheesecake for dessert.

Like meat and eggs, cheese is rich in proteins. It also has a high natural fat content. In the cooking process, the first thing to

happen is that the fat melts and runs out of the softening cheese. Then the proteins react to the heat by starting to coagulate. High temperatures coagulate the proteins so much that they harden. This is what gives a crisp finish to a dish sprinkled with grated cheese, and flashed under a red hot broiler. However, you don't want hard, tough pieces of cheese in fondue or other dishes.

If you overcook a dish such as macaroni and cheese, lasagne, pizza, or similar dishes with cheese as an essential ingredient, the cheese becomes stringy. It is then not only unpleasant to eat, but also highly indigestible.

For success in cheese cookery, the golden rule is the same as for eggs: gentle heat. For example, if you're adding cheese to a sauce that was started by the roux method, the

Right: tired of plain boiled vegetables? Try another way of doing them for a taste difference. This chart lists most of the methods you can use, and also shows which vegetables to do each way.

residual heat of the basic sauce is enough to melt the cheese. If possible, avoid reheating cheese dishes and keeping them warm for too long before serving. To speed up the melting of cheese in hot dips and fondues, grate the cheese finely. Do this, too, for pastries, biscuits, muffins, and other baked dishes containing cheese.

Processed cheese is especially formulated for cooking. It is made by mixing together and gently heating ripe and immature cheeses of the Cheddar type. An emulsifier is incorporated into the mixture to prevent the separation of the cheese proteins. Processed cheese won't get tough or stringy, but may not have the full flavor some prefer.

Cheeses have been known and made for almost 2000 years—for example, Cheshire cheese was exported to Rome from its area of production in the north of England during the Roman occupation of Britain. Cheese making arose as a means of preserving milk. Today, more than 400 different kinds of cheeses are known, and it is likely that there are others that have not become known outside their immediate area of origin.

Often cheeses are grouped as *hard-pressed*—such as Cheddar, Parmesan, Swiss, and Provalone; *semihard*—among them brick, Edam, Gouda, Oka, and Port Salut; *blue veined*—such as English Stilton, Danish blue, Roquefort, and Gorgonzola; *soft ripened*—including Camembert, Brie, Limburger, and Bel Paese; and *soft unripened*—notably cottage and cream cheeses.

When it comes to vegetables, many otherwise excellent cooks seem almost to leave them to their own devices. Although the main course may be seasoned, spiced, and sauced to perfection, the vegetables may be carelessly boiled, and not even dressed up with a knob of butter. What a contrast to those food perfectionists, the French, who often serve a beautifully prepared vegetable as a course on its own! Some of the sins of vegetable cookery can be reduced by an understanding of what happens when vegetables are cooked.

In scientific terms, the cooking process makes the cellulose in vegetables soften, and the starch in them gelatinize. As the cellulose softens, the vegetable loses its original crispness, but becomes more easily digestible. Cooking time is often dictated by the amount of cellulose the vegetable contains. Spinach, with little cellulose, cooks in a few minutes; carrots, well endowed with cellulose, may take ten times longer. Even the same vegetable takes different cooking times according to whether it is young or old. The older the vegetable, the more cellulose it contains, and the longer it needs to cook.

Cooking also affects the flavor of vegetables. Scientifically speaking, changes are brought about by the effect of heat on the flavoring constituents of the vegetable itself. The flavor may be enhanced by cooking—cooked greens, for example, have a much stronger flavor than raw ones. Strong flavored vegetables become more palatable by losing some of their pungent taste on cooking. Different cooking methods themselves also impart different flavors. Carrots slowly cooked in butter, for example, taste different from boiled carrots, and different again from the carrots you may add to the meat stew. In cooking, you can also add extra flavor with herbs, and spices.

How you normally cook vegetables often depends on which part of the world you live

# Cooking Vegetables

| | Boil | Broil | Steam | Bake | Fry | Deep Fry | Braise |
|---|---|---|---|---|---|---|---|
| Carrots | | | | | | | |
| Peas | | | | | | | |
| Brussels Sprouts | | | | | | | |
| Cauliflower | | | | | | | |
| Broccoli | | | | | | | |
| Cabbage | | | | | | | |
| Spinach | | | | | | | |
| Green Beans | | | | | | | |
| Lima Beans | | | | | | | |
| Beets | | | | | | | |
| Parsnips | | | | | | | |
| Sweet Potatoes | | | | | | | |
| Potatoes | | | | | | | |
| Squash | | | | | | | |
| Zucchini | | | | | | | |
| Tomatoes | | | | | | | |
| Mushrooms | | | | | | | |
| Turnips | | | | | | | |
| Rutabagas | | | | | | | |
| Celery | | | | | | | |
| Egg Plant | | | | | | | |
| Peppers | | | | | | | |
| Artichokes | | | | | | | |
| Asparagus | | | | | | | |
| Onions | | | | | | | |
| Corn | | | | | | | |

in, or how your own mother cooked them. Many Europeans cook vegetables in stock rather than water, and frequently add extra fat to the cooked vegetables—it may be olive oil in Italy, pork fat in Germany, unsalted butter in France. The English like to braise root vegetables around a roast in the oven.

Most cooks simply cook vegetables for as long as it takes to achieve the desired flavor and texture. Tenderness is important, but with regard to food value, vegetables should retain a little "bite", or slightly crisp texture. In order to preserve the precious vitamin C in green vegetables, and the nutrients in all vegetables, it is important to cook them just long enough for the vegetables to become tender, and then serve and eat them as soon as possible. Overcooked vegetables lose their fresh delicate flavor, and also their attractive color. Long cooking, keeping warm for a long time, or reheating vegetables can destroy all the vitamin C you would normally get. No one finds khaki-colored cabbage appetizing, and the strong flavor developed in overcooked cabbage is less than tasty.

We have already mentioned that cooking time very much depends on the amount of cellulose found in a vegetable. Cooking times are also dictated by the flavor of a vegetable. Mild flavored vegetables, such as peas, beans, spinach, corn, asparagus, globe artichokes, tomatoes, zucchini, new carrots, and beets, need to be cooked for the minimum amount of time in order to retain their delicate flavor. It is always best to use the smallest possible amount of cooking liquid so as not to wash out the flavor. New potatoes, beets, and carrots develop the best flavor of all if they

Right: take a tip from the French and serve an appetizer of raw vegetables with French dressing and mayonnaise dips. It's called a "crudité" platter in France—and it's crunchy and good to eat in any language at all.

Left: who would want to eat the overcooked cabbage in the left-hand side of this dish? Not only is it off color and shrunk, but it also lacks taste and nutritional value.

are well scrubbed and cooked in their skins. After cooking, the skin can be slipped off easily, and the hot vegetables tossed in melted butter.

Strong-flavored vegetables of the cabbage family—including all varieties of cabbage, broccoli, Brussels sprouts, rutabagas, turnips, and kohlrabi—should be cooked in enough liquid to wash away some of their strong taste, but not so much that the excess water washes away their vitamins. A reliable way of estimating the right amount of water for green vegetables is to use only the amount that, when boiling rapidly, will just bubble up and over the vegetables.

Strong-flavored vegetables of the onion family need long, slow cooking in plenty of liquid to reduce their somewhat overpowering taste. If you choose to boil them, use plenty of liquid, but simmer, don't actually boil. High temperature can cause the further development of strong tastes. If you plan to flavor soup, stock, sauce, or stuffing with onions, lightly sauté them in butter first. If you use raw onions, even though very finely chopped, their pungent taste can overpower the other flavoring ingredients your recipe calls for. Baked or roasted onions are good served around a roast, but always *blanch* them—that is, cook lightly in a large amount of rapidly boiling water—before baking them.

Never, never add bicarbonate of soda to vegetables to keep them green. You will instantly destroy all the vitamin C content. Rapidly cooked greens, served immediately, will retain all their attractive color without bicarbonate of soda. Overcooking is mainly responsible for loss of color, and bitter flavor.

# Themes and Variations
# 3

The old saying that "there's nothing new under the sun" applies aptly to cooking, for, the more you cook, the more you realize that most recipes fall into certain set patterns. Although countless new recipes are published each year in cookbooks, magazines, and newspapers, you will find that few are, in fact, new at all. They are more likely to be a different, or original, slant on an old familiar dish.

If you can cook one basic dish perfectly, the door is wide open for a number of dishes that look and taste different, but are simply variations on that basic recipe. For example, Lancashire hot pot, Hungarian goulash, and Indian curry are all stews. Once you know the method for making a stew, you can change the seasonings, flavoring ingredients, and liquids to produce the famous national dishes of the world that fall into the stew category—whether they are called a stew by name or not.

You can be a master cook if you make yourself familiar with fundamental cooking procedures such as creaming, beating, folding in, sautéing, braising, scalding, and so on. With a knowledge of how to do it, and some actual practice at it, you're all set to tackle any recipe—even those that sound somewhat complicated.

In the following pages you will find 12 selected recipes, each one chosen because it is a master formula that can be easily varied. In fact, variations are given as well. With them, you can cook a simple, delicious meal for the family, or a more sumptuous, festive meal for a dinner party.

Don't stop at these variations, though. Try your own. When you can add a dash of this or that to vary a basic recipe, you will begin to know the joys of creative cooking.

Right: the more you cook, the more you will find that most "new" recipes are simply variations on a few basic ones. Master the basics and you'll also find how easy—and how much fun—it can be to keep coming up with dishes that both look and taste temptingly different.

# *White Sauce*

Ingredients (for about 1 cup)
*2 tablespoons butter*
*2 tablespoons flour*
*1 cup milk*
*½ teaspoon salt*
*Pepper*

1. Melt butter in a small saucepan over low heat.
2. Add flour. Continue to cook, stirring constantly until the mixture—known as the "roux"—becomes frothy and leaves the bottom of the pan easily. At this stage the roux will have a slightly gritty texture.
3. Remove from heat and gradually beat in the milk.
4. Return to heat, and cook, stirring constantly, until sauce thickens enough to coat the back of the mixing spoon.
5. Add salt and pepper to taste.

Note: this is a medium sauce; for a thin one, use 1 tablespoon each of butter and flour; for a thick sauce, use 3 tablespoons each of butter and flour.

Above: melting the butter over low heat.

Above: adding the flour while stirring.

Below: beating in the milk off the heat.

Above: stirring constantly to thicken sauce.

Above: making cheese sauce, which is simply a variation of white sauce. To do it, add 1 cup of mild grated cheese—such as Swiss—to hot white sauce, and stir until the cheese melts. Add the seasoning after the cheese.

Above: topped with a smooth and creamy cheese sauce, broccoli looks and tastes better than usual.

# *Mayonnaise*

Ingredients (for about $1\frac{1}{4}$ cups)
*2 egg yolks*
*$\frac{1}{2}$ teaspoon prepared mustard*
*$\frac{1}{2}$ teaspoon salt*
*$\frac{1}{8}$ teaspoon pepper*
*$\frac{1}{2}$ teaspoon sugar*
*1 cup olive oil, vegetable oil, or half-and-half olive and vegetable oils*
*2 tablespoons wine vinegar, or*
*1 tablespoon wine vinegar and*
*1 tablespoon lemon juice*
*1 to 2 tablespoons light cream (if needed)*

Above: beating in oil *drop by drop* after egg yolks have been well beaten and seasoned.

1. Have all ingredients at room temperature. Beat egg yolks thoroughly in a small bowl.
2. Add mustard, salt, pepper, and sugar, and mix well.
3. *Drop by drop* add oil, beating thoroughly after each addition. When mixture becomes thick, opaque, and almost white, oil can be added a little more quickly.
4. When all the oil is incorporated and the mixture is smooth, beat in the vinegar, or vinegar and lemon juice.
5. If mayonnaise is too thick, add the cream.

Above: adding oil faster at a certain point.

*Variations:*
Tartare Sauce
To 1 cup mayonnaise, add
1 tablespoon chopped sweet pickles
1 tablespoon chopped capers
1 tablespoon chopped parsley
1 tablespoon minced onion
1 tablespoon chopped green or pimento-stuffed olives (optional)

Thousand Island Dressing
To 1 cup mayonnaise, add
2 tablespoons chili sauce
2 tablespoons minced green pepper
1 tablespoon chopped parsley
1 teaspoon grated onion

Above: beating in vinegar and/or lemon juice.

Above: use your rich homemade mayonnaise in an egg salad for lunch or supper, and watch the smiles of pleasure its special taste will bring.

Right: some people like mayonnaise as the basis of a light cocktail-type sauce used over shrimp.

# French Dressing

Ingredients (for one salad for 4–6)
*2 tablespoons vinegar, or mixture of vinegar and lemon juice*
*$\frac{1}{4}$ teaspoon salt*
*$\frac{1}{8}$ to $\frac{1}{4}$ teaspoon dry mustard (optional)*
*6 tablespoons olive or salad oil*
*Big pinch pepper*

1. In a small bowl, beat vinegar with salt and optional mustard until salt dissolves.
2. Add oil slowly, beating in well.
3. Season with pepper.

Alternative method:
Put all ingredients into a screw top jar, or one with a tight fitting cover, and shake vigorously to mix.

Note: this recipe gives the usual proportion of one part vinegar to three parts oil. The proportion can be altered to taste, but start with at least $\frac{1}{2}$ tablespoon vinegar. Mix the dressing with the salad just before serving for best results.

*Variations:*
Add any of the following—
1 crushed or finely chopped clove garlic
1 tablespoon finely chopped green onions
1 teaspoon finely chopped chives
1 tablespoon finely chopped mixed fresh herbs of your choice
2 softboiled egg yolks and a little chopped tarragon

Above: adding vinegar to salt in a small bowl.

Above: adding oil to be beaten in bit by bit.

Below: seasoning with pepper in the last step.

Above: a fast and easy way to make French dressing is to put all ingredients into a tight-lidded jar, and shake until mixed thoroughly.

Right: the perfect use for your delicious French dressing—a mixed salad containing lettuce, cucumbers, and tomatoes.

# Shirred Eggs

Ingredients (for each serving)
*1 or 2 eggs (1 for a first course; 2 for lunch or supper)*
*2 tablespoons butter, approximately*
*Salt and pepper*
*1 tablespoon light cream*

1. Preheat oven to 375°F.
2. Butter thickly small ovenproof dishes or custard cups, and heat them in the oven for a few minutes.
3. Break 1 or 2 eggs into each dish. Season with salt and pepper to taste.
4. Add 1 tablespoon of cream to each dish, and dot with butter.
5. Place dishes in baking pan, and add enough water to come halfway up the sides.
6. Bake for 8–10 minutes, until eggs have set.
7. Wipe dishes dry, and serve on big plate with buttered toast.

*Variations:*

With Vegetables
Break eggs on top of a dish lined with any lightly cooked vegetable or combination of vegetables—choose from green beans, eggplant, spinach, zucchini, sweet red peppers, mushrooms, or baked beans, for example.

With Meat
Break eggs on top of a dish lined with corn beef hash, chopped chicken, ground round steak, hamburger, or bacon or ham slices. Note: use either individual dishes with 1 or 2 eggs, or one large dish with 4 to 8 eggs. If a large dish, bake at 350°F for 20 minutes.

Piquant Shirred Eggs
Add any of the following: fresh chives, tarragon, or chervil; a dash of tabasco or cayenne pepper; a pinch of garlic powder, curry powder, or celery salt.

Party Shirred Eggs
1. Separate whites and yolks.
2. Beat whites stiffly, and spoon into dishes.
3. Drop yolk into center of beaten whites.
4. Season with salt and pepper to taste, add a tablespoon of light cream, and sprinkle with Parmesan cheese.
5. Bake as in basic recipe.

Above: thickly buttering ovenproof dishes.

Above: breaking eggs into separate dishes.

Above: spooning light cream over the eggs.

Above: pouring water into the baking pan.

Left: shirred eggs look so appetizing with a firm yolk in a creamy surrounding.
Above: for a party dish variation—drop egg yolks into stiffly beaten egg whites, add salt and pepper, and sprinkle with grated Parmesan cheese. Bake as for shirred eggs.

# Poached Fish Fillets

Ingredients (for 4)
*1 small onion, sliced*
*2 pounds fish fillets, skinned*
*2 tablespoons butter*
*½ pound mushrooms, sliced*
*½ cup dry white wine*
*½ cup water*
*Few bay leaves*

For sauce:
*2 tablespoons butter*
*2 tablespoons flour*
*Salt and pepper*
*¼ cup cream*
*1 ounce grated Swiss cheese*
*Few sliced tomatoes (optional, for garnish)*

1. Preheat oven to 350°F.
2. Lay half the onions in the bottom of an oval or oblong ovenproof dish. Arrange fish

Above: arranging sautéed mushrooms on fish.

fillets on top, either flat, folded, or rolled up. Season with salt and pepper to taste, and lay the rest of the onions on top of the fish.
3. In half the butter, lightly sauté the sliced mushrooms; arrange them on top of the fish.
4. Combine wine and water and pour over fish. Add bay leaves, and dot with second half of butter.
5. Cover dish and bake in a moderate oven, 350°F, for 10–15 minutes.
6. Drain off liquid carefully, reserve, and keep fish warm.
7. Make a roux with the butter and flour (refer to White Sauce, page 58). Add the reserved cooking liquid, stirring constantly until it thickens. Season with salt and pepper to taste, and add the cream. Cook a little longer to blend and make smooth.
8. Pour sauce over fish.
9. Sprinkle top with grated cheese and place under a hot broiler for two or three minutes to brown the top. Garnish with sliced tomatoes if desired.

*Variations:*
With Vegetables
Put a layer of a lightly cooked vegetable, or combination of vegetables, in the bottom of the baking dish, and poach the fish on top.
With Lemon Sauce
Add lemon juice to the sauce, and serve the fish with a few sliced lemons on top.
With Seafood
Add a few peeled shrimp, pieces of lobster, or halved scallops to the fish during poaching, and serve with an anchovy sauce.

Above: pouring combined wine and water over.

Above: covering the casserole for baking.

Above: draining off the liquid for the sauce.

Above: garnishing with a few sliced tomatoes.

Right: lightly browned on top, beautifully creamy inside, this fish dish is bound to get compliments from all.

# Chicken Fricassee

Above: browning the chicken parts in the fat.

Ingredients (for 6)
*5-pound stewing chicken, cut up*
*$\frac{1}{4}$ cup vegetable oil or other cooking fat*
*Boiling water to cover*
*$\frac{1}{2}$ small onion, sliced*
*1 small carrot, sliced*
*Few tops or stalks celery*
*Bay leaf*
*3 peppercorns or $\frac{1}{8}$ teaspoon pepper*
*2 teaspoons salt*

For sauce:
*$\frac{1}{4}$ cup butter*
*$\frac{1}{4}$ cup flour*
*2 cups liquid, either all broth from the cooked chicken, or a mixture of broth and milk, or broth and cream*
*Salt and pepper*
*Few drops of lemon juice or Worcestershire sauce*

1. Melt fat in a deep pan.
2. Add the chicken parts and brown evenly on all sides, using more fat if necessary.
3. Add boiling water to cover.
4. Add the onion, celery, carrot, bay leaf, and pepper. Cover and let simmer over low heat for 45 minutes.
5. Add salt and continue cooking until the chicken is tender, about 45 minutes more.
6. Remove from heat and let stand a few minutes; spoon fat off the surface. Remove the chicken and keep it warm.
7. Melt the butter in a small saucepan, and blend in the flour, as for White Sauce, page 58.
8. Add the cooking liquid slowly, stirring constantly, and, still stirring, heat to the boiling point to thicken. Season to taste with salt and pepper, and add the lemon juice or Worcestershire sauce.
9. Pour some of the sauce over the chicken, and pass the rest in a bowl.

*Variations:*
Chicken Pie
Follow the recipe for Chicken Fricassee, but do not brown the chicken first. After the meat is tender, remove the skin and bones. Place chicken in a baking dish not more than 3 inches deep, adding cooked vegetables—potatoes, peas, or carrots—if desired. Pour the sauce over the chicken, and cool to room temperature. (Do not chill.) Roll out plain pastry (see page 78), and fit it over the chicken, making cuts in it to let out steam as the pie bakes. Bake 10 minutes at 450°F. Reduce heat to 350° and bake 15 minutes longer, or until top is light brown.

Above: adding seasonings before simmering.

Above: spooning fat off the cooled surface.

Above: adding the lemon juice to the sauce.

Above: pouring some sauce over the chicken.

Right: tender and succulent, chicken fricassee is more de-licious because of the sauce made with its own cooking liquid.

# *Beef Stew*

Ingredients (for 4)
*2 large onions, chopped*
*2 cloves garlic, finely chopped*
*2 tablespoons cooking oil*
*2 tablespoons flour mixed with*
*½ teaspoon salt*
*⅛ teaspoon pepper*
*¼ teaspoon dry mustard*
*2 pounds stewing beef cut into 1-inch cubes*
*2 cups stock*
*4 medium carrots*
*½ teaspoon sage*
*½ teaspoon thyme*
*1 tablespoon chopped parsley (optional)*

1. Preheat oven to 325°F.
2. In a skillet, sauté onion and garlic in oil until onion begins to soften.
3. Trim and dry meat; toss in seasoned flour.
4. Brown meat in skillet with onion and garlic.
5. Add stock, and bring to boil, stirring well.
6. Transfer contents to 8-cup casserole; add quartered carrots and spices.
7. Cook in oven at 325°F for 2 to 2½ hours, or until beef is very tender.
8. Adjust seasoning and sprinkle top of stew with chopped parsley if desired.

*Variations:*
Burgundy beef
Beef Stew ingredients PLUS
1 cup red wine
1 tablespoon tomato paste
4 bay leaves
¼ teaspoon thyme
¼ teaspoon oregano
½ lb. small white onions
½ lb. button mushrooms

Note: omit chopped onion and 1 cup of stock from basic recipe. The first step will be to sauté garlic in oil. Follow the other steps, but cook stew for 1½ hours only. Then add onions and mushrooms, and cook for remaining time.

Above: sautéeing onion and garlic in oil.

Goulash
Beef Stew ingredients PLUS
2 tablespoons paprika
1 cup tomato juice
¼ teaspoon carraway seeds
4 bay leaves
1 lb. tomatoes, skinned and sliced, or canned
1 carton sour cream

Note: omit pepper and 1 cup of stock from basic recipe. Add the paprika before any liquids, sprinkling it onto the browned meat, blending it in well, and cooking for 2 to 3 minutes more. Add the tomatoes after bringing liquids to the boil. Stir in sour cream just before serving.

Above: tossing meat in the seasoned flour.

Above: browning meat with onion and garlic.

Above: adding stock to provide some liquid.

Above: seasoning the meat and vegetables.

Right: hearty, filling, and flavorful will be the verdict when you serve this beef stew.

# Scalloped Potatoes

Ingredients (for 4)
*1½ pounds potatoes*
*1 clove garlic*
*¼ cup butter*
*1 teaspoon salt*
*⅛ teaspoon pepper*
*½ cup grated Swiss cheese*
*1 cup boiling milk*

1. Preheat oven to 425°F.
2. Peel potatoes, slice thin, and place in a bowl of cold water.
3. Rub the inside of a shallow casserole with cut garlic, and smear it with part of the butter.
4. Drain potatoes, and dry in a cloth.
5. Spread half of them in the casserole, and add half the cheese, salt, and pepper. Do the same with the other half of the potatoes, cheese, salt, and pepper. Dot the top with remaining butter.
6. Pour in the boiling milk.
7. Bake at 425°F for 20 to 30 minutes, or until all milk has been absorbed and top is nicely browned.

Above: slicing the potatoes thin and even.

*Variations:*

With Tuna
Arrange flaked tuna fish between layers of potatoes, sprinkling it with ½ teaspoon finely grated lemon rind.

With Onions and Carrots
Chop 1 medium onion fine, and sauté in 1 tablespoon of butter until soft. Slice 4 large carrots thin, and blanch in boiling water for 5 minutes. Place these between potato layers.

With Onions and Tomatoes
Prepare onions as above. Chop 1 pound of skinned tomatoes coarsely, mix with onions, and season with thyme, marjoram, or parsley. Add between layers of potatoes. Use ½ cup tomato juice and ½ cup milk instead of all milk.

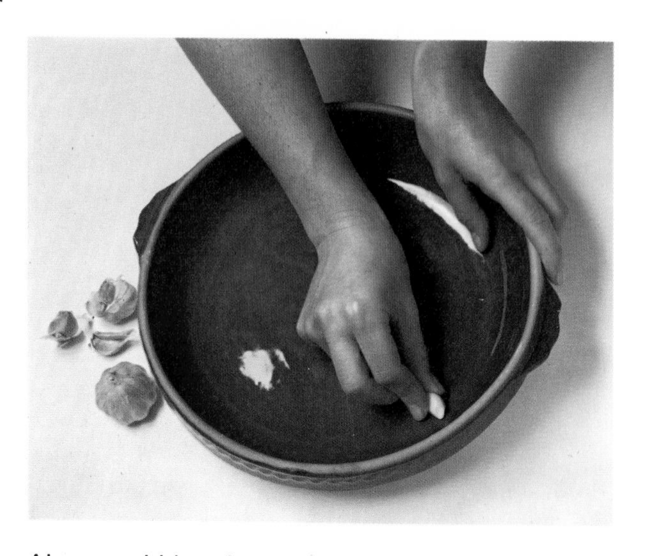

Above: rubbing the casserole with garlic.

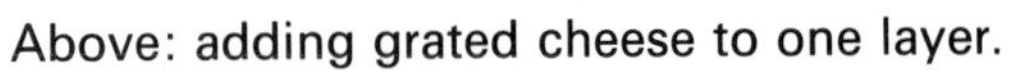

Above: adding grated cheese to one layer.

Above: pouring boiling milk into the dish.

Above: potato lovers love potatoes even more when they are baked and served this delicious way.

# *Cheese Soufflé*

Ingredients (for 4)
*6 tablespoons butter*
*$\frac{1}{2}$ cup flour*
*$1\frac{1}{4}$ cups milk*
*$\frac{1}{4}$ teaspoon salt*
*dash pepper*
*$\frac{1}{2}$ teaspoon prepared mustard*
*$\frac{1}{4}$ teaspoon ground nutmeg*
*3 large eggs, separated*
*$\frac{1}{2}$ cup Parmesan cheese, finely grated*
*$\frac{1}{2}$ cup Swiss cheese, finely grated*

1. Preheat oven to 400°F.
2. Butter well a 5-cup soufflé dish.
3. Make a White Sauce (page 58) with butter, flour, milk, salt, and pepper. Add mustard and nutmeg and blend well.
4. Allow sauce to cool slightly; cover well with wet waxed paper to avoid skinning. When sauce has cooled, beat in egg yolks.
5. Beat egg whites until they hold a peak well, and are stiff but not dry.
6. Fold whites into sauce very carefully, and transfer mixture to soufflé dish.
7. Run handle of a spoon around edge of soufflé to ensure even rising.
8. Bake at 400°F for 40 to 45 minutes. The top of the soufflé should be golden brown and firm, and a skewer run into the middle should come out clean.

Above: buttering the soufflé dish thoroughly.

*Variations:*
Note: additions are made after beating in egg yolks.

Spinach and Ham Soufflé
Cook a package of frozen spinach and drain well. Add with 4 ounces chopped ham.

Seafood soufflé
Add 4 ounces well drained frozen shellfish and 1 teaspoon anchovy paste.

Chicken Soufflé
Add 4 ounces chopped cooked chicken and 1 teaspoon finely chopped parsley

Above: adding mustard and nutmeg to sauce.

Above: folding the beaten egg whites in.

Below: running spoon handle around the edge.

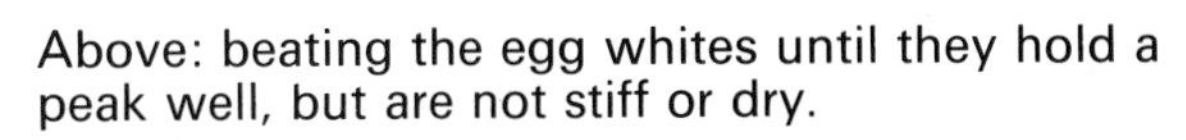

Above: beating the egg whites until they hold a peak well, but are not stiff or dry.

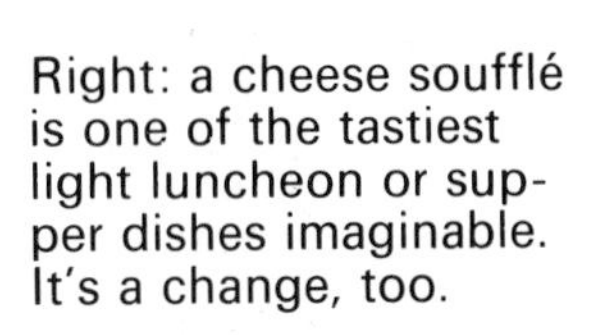

Right: a cheese soufflé is one of the tastiest light luncheon or supper dishes imaginable. It's a change, too.

# Chocolate Mousse

Ingredients (for 4)
*4 ounces semisweet chocolate (chips, or 1-ounce squares)*
*2 tablespoons softened butter*
*4 eggs, separated*

1. Melt chocolate in top of double boiler over low heat, or in a bowl standing in a pan of simmering water.
2. When chocolate has melted, stir in butter.
3. Off heat, beat in egg yolks thoroughly, and transfer mixture to a large bowl.
4. Beat egg whites till stiff but not dry.
5. Fold whites into chocolate mixture.
6. Pour into serving dish or individual serving dishes. Chill. Serve topped with whipped cream.

Garnish, if desired, with grated chocolate, crystalized ginger, or tiny peppermint creams.

*Variations:*
Add any of the following to melted chocolate at the same time as the butter:
1 tablespoon rum or brandy
1 tablespoon Grand Marnier, Tia Maria, or Curaçao
1 tablespoon orange or grapefruit juice
A few drops peppermint essence

Above: melting chocolate in double boiler.

Above: adding the butter to the chocolate.

Below: beating in egg yolks, done off heat.

Above: folding in the beaten egg whites.

Above: transferring the mousse to glasses.

Right: rich and creamy, this chocolate mousse makes a dessert that is special—and only you know how easy it was!

# *Pastry*

Ingredients (for 9-inch two-crust pie)
*2 cups pastry flour or 1¾ cups all-purpose flour*
*1 teaspoon salt*
*⅔ cup vegetable shortening, lard, or a combination of ⅓ cup lard and ⅓ cup butter*
*½ cup ice water*

1. Sift flour and salt into a mixing bowl.
2. Cut in the shortening with a pastry blender, blending fork, or two knives (holding one in each hand) until mixture resembles coarse meal with particles the size of peas.
3. Sprinkle the ice water over the mixture by tablespoonfuls, working it in with a fork just till you can form the dough into a ball. (You may not use all the water.) Handle the dough as little and as lightly as possible.
4. Wrap the dough in wax paper or foil and chill.
5. When chilled, divide the dough into two parts, one slightly larger, and return the smaller part to the refrigerator.
6. Dust a pastry board or cloth with a very small amount of flour, and place the larger ball of chilled dough on it. (This will be the bottom crust.) Flatten the ball slightly with a light tap or a few strokes of the rolling pin.
7. Roll with quick, light strokes, always working from the center, and keeping the dough as even in thickness as possible—it should be about ⅛-inch thick. To keep it from sticking, lift the dough occasionally with a broad spatula, and dust very lightly with flour.
8. Line a 9-inch pie pan, and proceed with the filling and top crust.

Note: speed and light handling are essential for successful pastry. Experienced cooks can blend the flour and shortening with their fingers, working so fast that the shortening doesn't even soften. Beginners usually blend ingredients too thoroughly—remember, they just have to hold together in a ball.

Above: sifting the flour and salt together.

Above: cutting shortening into flour mixture.

Above: sprinkling ice water to be worked in.

Above: forming the dough gently into a ball.

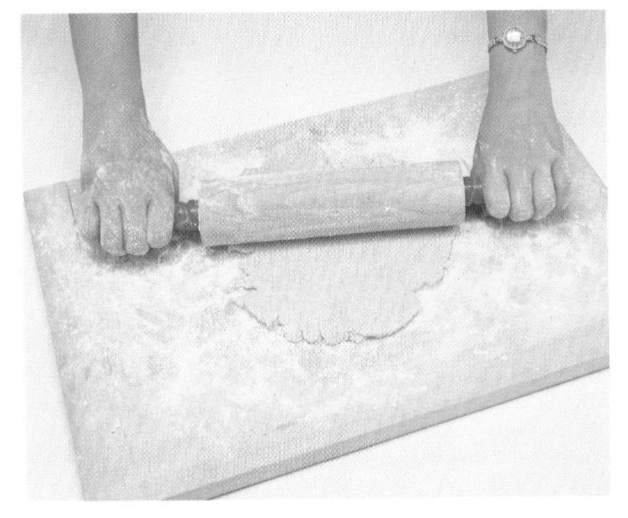

Above: starting to roll dough from center.

Above: nearing the end of the rolling out.

Right: isn't a yummy apple pie almost everyone's favorite? Master this plain pastry, and your pies—whatever the filling—will get cheers whenever you serve them.

# *Muffins*

Ingredients (for 12)
*1 $\frac{3}{4}$ cups all-purpose flour or 2 cups pastry flour*
*3 teaspoons baking powder*
*$\frac{1}{2}$ teaspoon salt*
*2 tablespoons sugar*
*2 eggs, slightly beaten*
*1 cup milk*
*$\frac{1}{4}$ cup melted butter*

1. Preheat oven to 400°F.
2. Sift flour, baking powder, salt, and sugar into a mixing bowl.
3. In another bowl, mix eggs, milk, and melted butter.
4. Pour the liquid mixture over the flour mixture, and stir only enough to dampen the flour. (Batter is supposed to be lumpy.)
5. Spoon into two buttered 6-muffin tins, or one 12-muffin tin, filling about two-thirds full.
6. Bake at 400°F 15 to 20 minutes, until tops are golden brown.

Above: sifting the dry ingredients together.

*Variations:*

Blueberry Muffins
Reserve $\frac{1}{4}$ cup of the flour, sprinkle it over 1 cup blueberries, and set aside. Use $\frac{1}{2}$ cup sugar in the batter. Stir berries into batter last.

Bacon Muffins
Use bacon fat as the shortening, and add 3 tablespoons crumbled cooked bacon to batter.

Date or Raisin Muffins
Add $\frac{1}{2}$ cup sliced pitted dates or $\frac{1}{4}$ cup raisins.

Pecan Muffins
Use $\frac{1}{4}$ cup sugar. Add $\frac{1}{2}$ cup chopped pecans. After filling tins, sprinkle with sugar, cinnamon, and more nuts.

Orange Muffins
Add $\frac{3}{4}$ cup candied orange peel, cut in small pieces.

Above: mixing liquid and butter separately.

Above: mixing the liquid and flour mixtures.

Above: spooning muffin batter into the tin.

Above: hot muffins make a leisurely Sunday breakfast special—yet they're easy and quick to make.

# Roasting Meat

Right: how long a roast takes to get done depends on several variables, from how you like it, to the size, to the amount of outside and inside fat in the meat. That's why any timetable can only be the merest guide.

There are no hard and fast rules on how long meats should be roasted because of so many variables. For example, do you like meat rare, medium, or well done? There can be a time difference of one hour between rare and well done for a four-pound rolled rib roast. Timing also depends on oven temperatures. A high temperature of up to 400°F gets the roast done faster, and gives an attractive brown crispness outside; but the inside then tends to be rather dry, and shrinkage increases.

The tenderness of your roast also affects the cooking time. An ultra-tender tenderloin weighing between four and six pounds should be adequately cooked in less than an hour. Tougher cuts, naturally, will take longer. Likewise, a thick rolled roast takes longer to cook than a thinner roast with the bone in. (The bone itself helps the meat to cook more evenly, and to retain moisture.)

Therefore, roasting times given in recipes should be considered only as a guide. They are generally calculated on the weight of the meat, so be sure you keep a record of how much the roast you are going to do weighs. Keep in mind, too, that most cooks find that roasting at 325° to 350°F gives the best results. At this moderate temperature, shrinkage is kept to a minimum, and juiciness to a maximum.

When you estimate your cooking time on the basis of minutes-per-pound, allow 15 to 20 minutes for the roast to "rest" out of the oven after cooking. You will find that the meat is much easier to carve, and, unless the roast is very small, it will retain enough heat to be right for serving. The resting time also gives you time to make gravy, or do other last minute finishing up.

Rib roasts are the most popular cut of beef for roasting in the U.S. The best rib roast is cut from the loin end. It is especially tender, and has a greater proportion of lean meat. Rib roasts from the chuck or shoulder end are slightly tougher, and have a smaller eye of lean meat. Each of these cuts may be prepared as: a standing 10-inch rib roast with long rib bones and some back bone; a standing 7-inch rib roast with some of the rib and back bone removed; a rolled rib roast—boned, rolled, and secured with string.

The muscle from the rib roast may be removed and sold on its own as rib eye roast, or Delmonico. This is similar in appearance, though usually not so tender, as the tenderloin, which is the most expensive roasting cut of all. The tenderloin is the lean muscle cut from beneath the backbone in the loin section.

Rump or rolled rump can also be roasted, although pot roasting is usually more suitable because of its relative toughness.

The three roasts usually cut from the loin section are the most popular pork cuts. These are usually sold and cooked on the bone, but they are often boned and rolled in Europe. You can bone such roasts at home yourself if you like; it makes the roast easier to carve. The sirloin roast that includes the tenderloin is generally said to be the best pork roast. Shoulder roasts, such as the Boston Butt and picnic, are economical and tasty. They may be sold with or without the bone in, but the cushion shoulder roast is usually boned.

Leg, or fresh ham, is another excellent pork roast. It may be cut into butt end, center cut, and shank half, and any of these may be boned and rolled.

For a special occasion, ask your butcher to prepare a crown roast.

Lamb roast cuts are similar to those of pork. If the leg roast has the sirloin attached, it is known as leg of lamb. Otherwise, the leg is divided into the sirloin roast and the shank half roast. Shoulder roasts are usually boned and rolled to allow easy carving.

A crown roast of lamb, usually of 14 ribs, is excellent company fare.

# *Roasting Timetable*

| Type of Cut | Oven Temperature | Minutes per pound | | | Reading on Meat Thermometer | | |
|---|---|---|---|---|---|---|---|
| | | Rare | Medium | Well Done | Rare | Medium | Well Done |
| **BEEF** | | | | | | | |
| Standing rib | 325° | 23–25 | 27–30 | 32–35 | 140° | 160° | 180° |
| Rolled rib | 325° | 28–30 | 32–35 | 40–45 | 140° | 160° | 180° |
| Sirloin, rump, eye of round | 325° | 18–20 | 22–25 | 30–35 | 140° | 160° | 180° |
| Tenderloin | 425° | 45 minutes to 1 hour total time | | | Usually served rare only | | |
| Note: there are two ways to get a crisp outside crust on roast beef. One is to start the roast at a high oven temperature, 450°, for 15 minutes, and reduce the heat to 325° for the rest of the cooking time. The other is to raise the temperature to 400° about 15 minutes before the roasting time is up, and baste the meat several times with the fat that has dripped into the roasting pan. | | | | | | | |
| **PORK** | | | | | | | |
| Loin | 350° | | | 45 | | | 185° |
| Shoulder | 350° | | | 50 | | | 185° |
| **LAMB** | | | | | | | |
| Leg, loin, shoulder | 325° | | 15–20 | 25–30 | | 150° | 180° |
| Crown | 325° | 2 hours total time | | | Usually served medium rare | | |
| **CHICKEN** | 325° | | | 25–30 | | | 180° |
| **TURKEY** | 325° | | | 20–25 | | | 180° |
| **DUCK** | 325° | | | 20–25 | | | 175° |
| **GOOSE** | 325° | | | 25–30 | | | 175° |

# When Things Go Wrong

# 4

Above: when a soufflé flops, you can only do one of two things—serve it as it is, or dump it and come up with a quick substitute. Before you give it up, though, remember that the taste probably hasn't suffered at all.

Left: it's ingenuity to the rescue when things go wrong—and we all have a failure of some kind or another from time to time. Here a cake that has caved in the middle is turned into a thing of beauty by filling the center with canned fruit, and trimming the edge with fancy whipped cream rosettes.

Your guests are chatting happily over drinks while you're finishing up the cream of asparagus soup for the appetizer. (You made it ahead of time except for adding the enrichment of eggs, butter, and cream.) Perhaps you forgot to taste it when you made it earlier, or perhaps you get a little absent-minded as you adjust the seasoning at this point. In any case, you taste it, and realize with a sinking feeling that it's disastrously salty. Here is one of those moments when things go wrong—and it's your immediate problem to set them right. Be comforted, however. You can usually do an acceptable salvage operation if you remain calm, and remember—or look up—a way of saving the situation.

Usually, too, most seeming calamities are little ones. It's not often that food is spoiled beyond recognition. In fact, some families prefer certain dishes that don't turn out quite as they should. You may be asked to bake a cake that is soggy, or pastry so crumbly that you can't cut it into neat slices, or turkey dressing that is dry.

In any case, it's a rare cook who doesn't have a minor crisis in the kitchen from time to time. Most of these cooking errors can be blamed on too much hastiness, interruptions, or distractions. For instance, after you broke away from your baking to answer the phone, can you remember whether or not you added the baking powder to the flour? Can you manage to divide your attention between a custard on the point of thickening just right, and your son on the point of howling over a lost toy?

Some cooks maintain that they do better when time is at a premium. Certainly pastry is best if made with a light, quick hand, and

Below: burned the Brussels sprouts? A quick way to take the burned taste out is to put the food in a clean pot, place a metal cap full of salt on top, and let sit a few minutes. Bottom: take care of a scorched pan immediately by soaking it in a strong salt solution.

a minimum of handling. Certainly a roast cooks more evenly when you don't open the oven door to look at it every 15 minutes or so. Stews, rich fruit cakes, and other dishes needing long, slow cooking, like a little healthy neglect—provided you're sure your oven is not overheating, or the simmer state is being maintained.

However, you have to keep a careful eye on dishes needing a short cooking time. Most vegetables, rice, and pasta cook in less than half an hour, for example, and they spoil with overcooking. To lessen the possibility of forgetting how long something has been cooking, most busy cooks find a kitchen timer invaluable. Its warning bell will remind you that a certain dish is at a critical stage, and so will help you coordinate a meal. You won't have to worry about overdoing the rice, which is difficult to get exactly right, if you do this: cook it until it is just slightly hard in the center. Drain it well, place in a well-buttered, shallow pan or dish, and cover with buttered foil. Put it in the lower part of a warm oven, and it will cook-and-keep for up to half an hour without overcooking.

Your biggest panic in the kitchen is probably burning food. Vegetables, especially those cooked in very little liquid, and rice, which absorbs its cooking liquid, are particularly prone to burning. If you're lucky, you catch it when only a thin layer of the food is burned. You can then simply use what is not scorched. When the burning is more extensive, however, the whole pan full of food develops a burned taste, even though it is not all scorched. One remedy you can try is to disguise the taste by adding a strongly flavored ingredient, such as barbecue sauce or curry powder. Another solution is to remove the food from the scorched pan, put it in a clean one, and place a small metal lid filled with salt on top of it. Cover and let sit for a few minutes. (Be sure to use a metal container for the salt—a ketchup bottle lid is just right.) Remember one other tip: uncover the pan of burned food, and set it in a bigger pan of cold water till the steam escapes. The burned taste should go with the steam.

Incidentally, treat a scorched pan immediately. Put a generous handful of coarse salt in the pan as soon as you have scraped out the burned food. Then fill the pan with cold water, and leave it to soak overnight. You will find that the strong salt solution usually gets rid of the burned remains.

Now let's go back to that oversalted soup of the first paragraph—or any too-salty food. Surprisingly, mashed potatoes are most useful in absorbing excessive saltiness. For a gravy, sauce, or soup that is too salty, sprinkle in a little instant mashed potatoes, and stir thoroughly. If you have some cold mashed potatoes on hand, beat them into the gravy, soup, or sauce. Of course, the potatoes will make any of these foods thicker, but that is generally preferable to being too salty. Oversalted vegetables, too, can be saved by the

Above: don't despair if you've oversalted the gravy. Stir in some instant mashed potatoes, and you'll repair the damage in a jiffy. The gravy will get thicker, of course, but no one will mind that too much.

Right: there's a shuddery moment when you wonder if your guests will know that you had to rescue the oversalted vegetable by adding lemon juice. But they'll never guess it!

addition of cooked potatoes, which you mash together with the vegetables. Other cures suggested for oversalted food include adding lemon juice, cream, or sugar.

Although some families like their meat well done, there is a stage of cooking that can only be described as "overdone". If your roast or stew has become dry and flavorless from overcooking, you can grind the meat, mix it with a thick but well-flavored sauce, and make it into meat loaf, pancake filling, meat balls, or meat patties. If, at the other extreme, you find your roast is almost raw when you start to carve it, here is a quick solution: slice the meat, place on a metal dish or in the roasting pan, and cook in the top of a hot oven (425°F) for 10 minutes, or under the broiler for about five minutes. Watch it all the time if it's under the broiler; it can burn quickly.

Always remember to taste food just before serving it, and to adjust the seasoning at this stage. It is difficult to judge the amount of salt, pepper, herbs, and spices a dish needs before the flavors of all the ingredients have blended together in cooking. For improving soups and gravies, keep a few different types of stock cubes in your cupboard, and add one —or part of one—if the soup or gravy seems somewhat tasteless. This works wonders to give more flavor. Remember, though, that stock cubes increase the saltiness of food. So don't use this flavoring method if it will make your soup or gravy oversalty. Instead, try wine, tomato paste, mustard, monosodium glutamate, or lemon juice—all are great flavor boosters.

In the chapter on the science of cooking, we tried to explain what happens in cooking meat, fish, cheese, eggs, and vegetables. When it comes to baking, though, it is difficult to know what is actually happening inside a cake, a loaf of bread, or a pie while it is in the oven. It is also hard to make last-minute adjustments to the flavor of a baked dish—although there must be some cooks who, at one time or another, have added the forgotten sugar through tiny holes made in the crust of their

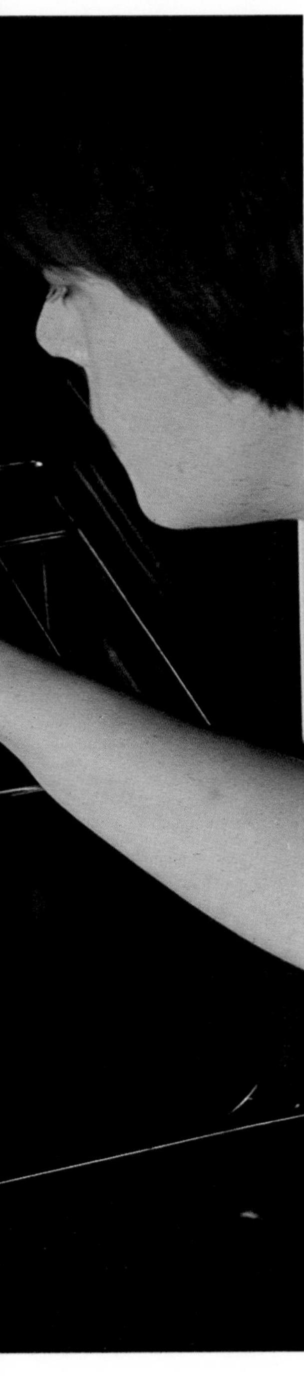

Left: oven temperatures have a bothersome way of varying from side to side on a shelf, and from shelf to shelf as well. Putting an oven thermometer in the very spot you're going to use is the best way of getting the exact heat you want.

finished pies—with no one the wiser!

The telling factor in all kinds of baking is the intimate relationship between flour, shortening, and eggs. We can judge this relationship by the different tastes and textures we achieve by varying the proportions of these ingredients for cakes, cookies, biscuits, bread, batter, and pastry. The quantity and type of leavening agent used also makes a great difference, as well as the techniques of mixing, beating, folding in, or whatever.

While you can do something immediate when you burn or oversalt food, you can do little except analyze what might have gone wrong when you have a baking failure. Still, this analysis can help you do a better—or perhaps perfect—job next time.

Often you cannot pinpoint exactly what you may have done incorrectly. For example, a book cannot tell you if you are properly creaming, beating, or folding in. You usually perfect these techniques with practice and experience. Remember also that oven temperatures are critical for most baking, but ovens are rarely perfect. Don't expect the same temperature in every part of your oven, even if the thermostat is set for the desired heat. For example, temperatures may vary slightly from side to side, and from front to back on a shelf, and the heat also varies between top, middle, and bottom shelves. You can make sure the temperature is accurate by putting an oven thermometer in the spot you intend to use for baking. Always preheat your oven so that the temperature gets a chance to come to the right level before you put anything in to bake.

As a general rule, use all ingredients at room temperature for baking. (Pastry is the big exception; all ingredients should be kept cool.) Accurate measuring is also vital to successful baking—even the professionals measure carefully.

Now lets look at some specific things that go wrong in baking and cooking, and find out what we can do about them—either at once, or next time around.

# *Pastry*

Above: when pastry sticks to the rolling pin, it could be that you rolled too hard.

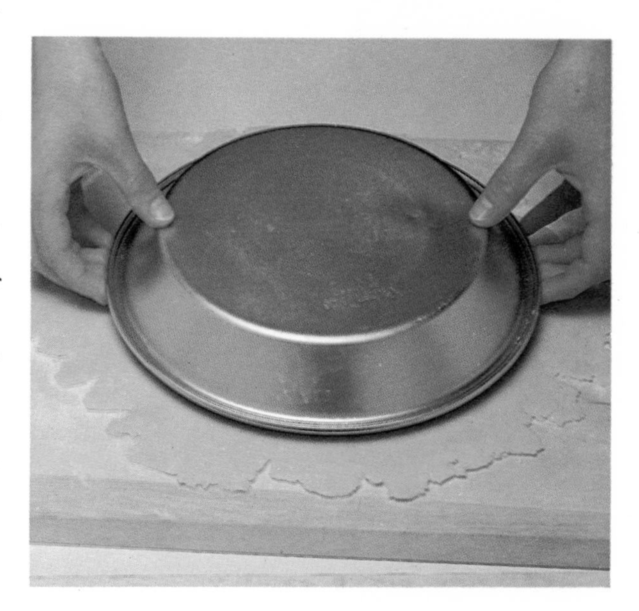

Above: pastry will fit the pan better if you roll it $1\frac{1}{2}$–2 inches larger than the pan.

*Problem:* pastry is too sticky to roll out.
*Possible causes:* handling too much. Rolling too hard. Working in a hot kitchen. Using a soft cake flour.
*Remedy:* first of all, use only all-purpose or pastry flour, and always keep ingredients cool. If it has gotten sticky, roll it into a ball and leave it in the refrigerator to harden for at least half an hour. When rolling out pastry, use light strokes in one direction only, starting from the center.
*Problem:* pastry is too crumbly.
*Possible causes:* adding too much fat. Using too little liquid to bind flour and shortening. Overmixing shortening with flour.
*Remedy:* lightly knead pastry until it becomes a little smoother. Then roll out very gently, pinching together the edges of any cracks if they appear. If impossible to roll at all, crumble it more and use it for a streusel or crumb topping.
*Problem:* pastry is tough and hard.
*Possible causes:* using too little fat. Adding too much liquid. Baking too slowly in an oven that was not hot enough. Handling too much or too roughly. Using too much flour to dust the board or rolling pin.
*Remedy:* none. The only thing that will help a little is to serve the pie hot instead of cold.
*Problem:* pastry shell shrinks from sides of pie plate.
*Possible causes:* adding too little fat. Overstretching the pastry when rolling it.
*Remedy:* avoid overstretching in the first place by handling gently. Allow pastry to rest in the refrigerator after rolling out, but before trimming the edges to fit the baking tin.
*Problem:* base of shell rises or bubbles.
*Possible causes:* failure to remove air by pressing pastry gently but firmly into pie plate. Not pricking well to prevent air pockets.
*Remedy:* prick base well with fork before baking. Fill unbaked shell with foil, and cover foil with dried beans or rice; remove foil and beans after shell has been baked and cooled.
*Problem:* bottom crust is damp and soggy.
*Possible causes:* bottom undercooked. Pie plate too thick. Oven not hot enough. Filling is very

Above: help prevent bubbling of a prebaked pie shell by pricking the bottom thoroughly.

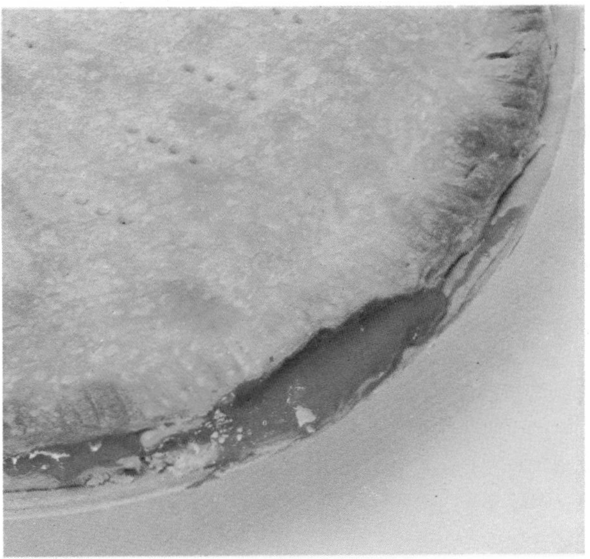

Above: a juicy filling might ooze out if you don't seal the double crust firmly.

Above: another bubble preventer is to fill and bake the shell with beans inside foil.

Above: pressing the two crusts together with a fork is a good way to seal them.

juicy. Pie baked on top shelf of oven.
*Remedy:* place pie plate on a cookie sheet to spread the oven heat evenly. Bake pies at 400° to 425°F in middle of oven. If fruit filling is likely to be very juicy, sprinkle one or two tablespoons of flour, cornstarch, or quick-cooking tapioca onto filling before fitting top crust.
*Problem:* juices drip out of pie while baking.
*Possible causes:* failure to brush edges of bottom crust with cold water before adding top crust. Failure to seal edges properly.
*Remedy:* make sure the edges are well sealed. The best way is to press the prongs of a fork or the handle of a spoon along the edges. A pastry wheel will also do the trick. As a precaution, do the same as for preventing a soggy bottom crust, above.

# Cakes

*Problem:* cake doesn't rise well, and texture is heavy and close.
*Possible causes:* measuring ingredients inaccurately. Using baking powder that is the wrong kind or too old. (Keep it in an airtight container, and replace every three months.) Using too little baking powder or baking soda. Not creaming shortening and sugar to the light, fluffy stage. Overbeating the batter after flour was added. Baking at wrong oven temperature.
*Remedy:* measure ingredients exactly. For example, don't pack flour or white sugar tight in the measuring cup. Be sure to preheat oven to right temperature. As a general rule, avoid mixing too much after adding flour.
*Problem:* cake rises unevenly.
*Possible causes:* baking at the side rather than in the middle of the oven. Failing to sift flour and baking powder or soda thoroughly. Not mixing flour in enough.
*Remedy:* use an oven thermometer to check on the correctness of temperature in different parts. The sides may be different from the middle; if so, bake in the middle part of the shelf. Don't put two layer cakes side by side. Sift flour and baking powder or soda at least three times together to distribute the leavening agent evenly.
*Problem:* cake rises in the middle.
*Possible causes:* using too much leavening agent. Baking at wrong oven temperature. Using the wrong size cake pan.
*Remedy:* measure all ingredients accurately, especially the leavening agent. Make sure oven temperature is correct and steady. It will also help to use the middle shelf for large cakes, and the top shelf for small cakes or cup cakes.

*Problem:* cake sinks in the middle.
*Possible causes:* opening the oven door too soon, or slamming the oven door. Taking out the cake before it was cooked in the middle.
*Remedy:* allow ample baking time before checking to see if the cake is done. Take care not to jar the cake suddenly.
*Problem:* cake is too dry.
*Possible causes:* adding too little shortening or

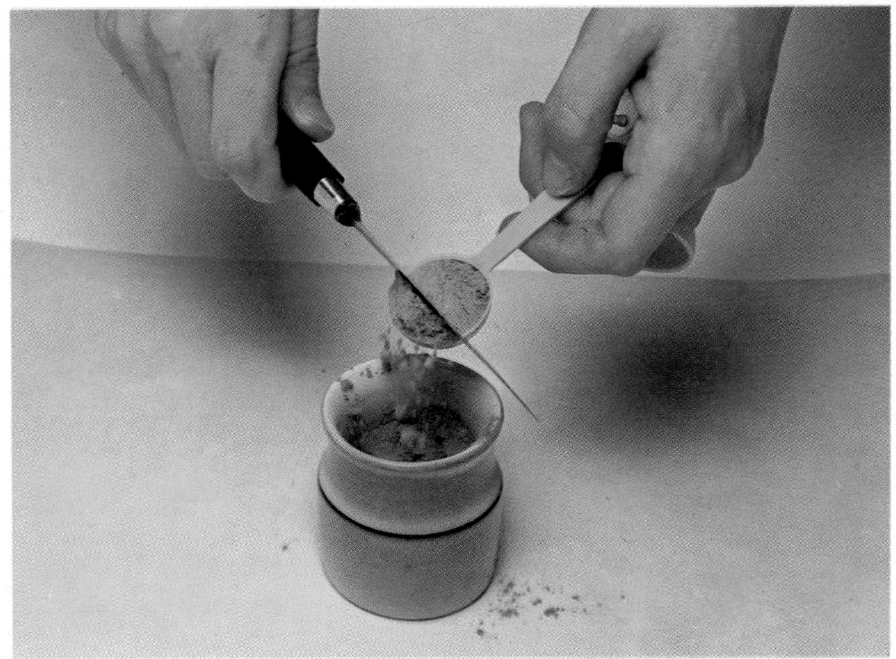

too few eggs. Baking too long or too slowly. Using insufficient liquid.
*Remedy:* remember that the less shortening and eggs a cake calls for, the drier it will be. However, a dry cake can be made more moist by replacing about one-third of the sugar called for with either corn syrup or molasses. Plain cakes don't keep well, so eat them quickly. Store in an airtight container for

Above: flour should never be packed down when measured, so the method illustrated on the left above and at the top right is one of the most accurate ways to get exact measurement. First, sift the flour directly into the measuring cup, allowing a generous extra amount to peak. Then, push the excess off straight across the top of the cup with the flat of a knife or a metal spatula. The same principle applies to measuring spices, baking powder or soda (above), but use something small for leveling.

only a short time, if it proves necessary.
*Problem:* top of cake is too dark.
*Possible causes:* placing the cake too near the top of the oven. Baking in too hot an oven. Using a bigger pan than recommended.
*Remedy:* if it is a rich cake needing long baking, cover the top with foil or thick brown paper halfway through the baking time.
*Problem:* top and sides of fruit cake are too brown.
*Possible causes:* using a very thin cake pan. Failing to line the pan with a double layer of waxed paper.
*Remedy:* always use good quality cake pans to help cakes brown evenly without burning. It also helps to tie a double layer of corrugated or brown wrapping paper around the outside of the pan. Use foil or paper on top halfway through, as above.
*Problem:* cake has a hard sugary crust.
*Possible causes:* using too much sugar. Using too large a cake pan. Overbaking or baking at too hot a temperature.
*Remedy:* measure ingredients carefully, and check oven temperature. Always use the right size cake pan, or make adjustments to the recipe to allow for a larger or smaller size.
*Problem:* cake has a speckled top or yellowish flecks throughout.
*Possible causes:* not sifting flour and leavening

Left: it's the start of something delicious coming out of your creative kitchen.
Below: maybe you produced the perfect muffin, as on the left, for a special family treat. If the muffins went askew, as shown on right, it could be that your oven temperature was too high.

agent thoroughly. Using the wrong amount or wrong kind of leavening agent.
*Remedy:* remember that thorough sifting of flour and leavening agent is important. Leavening agents can vary—there are several different kinds of baking powder, for example, or it may be baking soda that is called for.
*Problem:* fruit in a cake sinks to the bottom.
*Possible causes:* using too much liquid. Using very heavy fruit. Not drying the fruit properly before adding it. Not having the oven hot enough. Using a cake flour.
*Remedy:* always use completely dry fruit; if bought ready-to-use, it needs no further washing. Cut large pieces of dried fruit into small pieces. A harder flour than usual is best for rich fruit cakes—try a bread flour, in fact.
*Problem:* jelly roll cracks when being rolled.
*Possible causes:* using too large a cake pan. Overbaking it. Leaving it for too long before starting to roll it. Failing to line the baking pan with waxed paper.
*Remedy:* bake a jelly roll for only about 7–8 minutes at 425°F—the edges should not be allowed to get crisp. Turn out the cake on a sheet of paper covered with superfine sugar, and lying on a damp cloth. Cover with a clean dish towel as it cools. Cut off all outer edges with a sharp knife, spread with hot jam, and roll up while still slightly warm.

# Bread

*Problem:* bread doesn't rise well, and has a close texture.
*Possible causes:* adding too little yeast. Failing to knead the dough properly. Using too soft a flour. Leaving the dough to rise in too warm a place. Adding too much salt. Using too many enriching ingredients, such as eggs, sugar, or shortening.
*Remedy:* use bread flour if possible. Yeast is killed by too high a temperature, so it is often best to allow dough to rise at room temperature. The more enriching ingredients added, the less active the yeast will be for raising the dough; so go easy on eggs, etc.
*Problem:* top of loaf flips, or crust is badly cracked.
*Possible causes:* using too soft a flour. Not adding enough liquid. Not letting the dough rise enough. Putting too much dough in the loaf pan.
*Remedy:* try always to use bread flour for bread and cakes made with yeast. Rather than make a dough with too little liquid, make it slightly too wet, and adjust the consistency with more flour. Extra flour can easily be added, but not extra liquid. Allow dough to rise until it springs back instantly when gently pressed with a floured finger. Follow directions in recipes for filling loaf pans correctly.
*Problem:* bread has a sour or yeasty taste.
*Possible causes:* using too much yeast. Letting the dough rise too much so that it has to be rekneaded and allowed to rise again.
*Remedy:* use only the amount of yeast called for. Watch the second rising carefully, and make the above test for risen dough.
*Problem:* bread or yeasted cake has holes and uneven texture.
*Possible causes:* using too much yeast. Not kneading the dough enough before letting it rise either the first or second time. Leaving it too long before baking.
*Remedy:* use the right amount of yeast, and knead the dough well to distribute the yeast evenly. Bake as soon as possible after the dough has risen twice.
*Problem:* top of rising dough is dry and hard.
*Principal cause:* not covering the dough well during rising period.
*Remedy:* if the dough has skinned, cut it off; don't try to knead it back into the dough. Always cover rising dough. When letting breads rise in their baking pans, place the whole pan inside a greased plastic bag.
*Problem:* bread stales quickly and is crumbly.
*Possible causes:* not using the right amount of yeast. Letting the bread rise in too warm a place. Using soft flour instead of bread flour.
*Remedy:* be sure to use the right amount of yeast and the right kind of flour. Never try to hurry the rising process by putting the dough in an overwarm place.

Below right: bread hasn't risen, being about two-thirds the height of the other loaf shown. Among the tips for getting well risen bread are: use enough yeast; don't let the dough rise in too warm a place; go easy on enriching ingredients—eggs, sugar, shortening.

Although bread is easier to make than many think, things can go wrong—and here are some examples.

Right: the top of the loaf has flipped. One way you can avoid this is not to overfill pans.

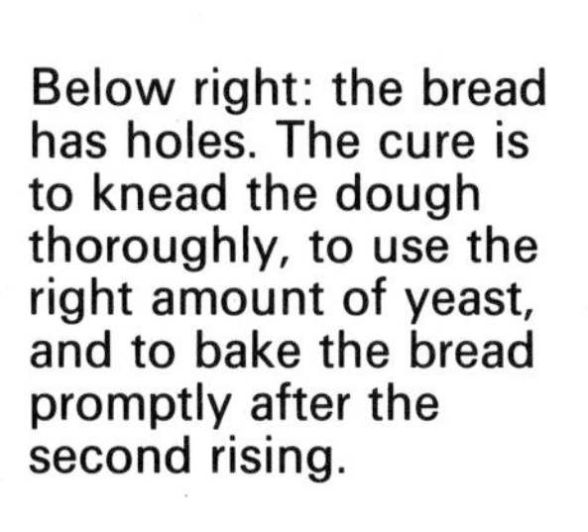

Below right: the bread has holes. The cure is to knead the dough thoroughly, to use the right amount of yeast, and to bake the bread promptly after the second rising.

# Sauces

*Problem:* sauce is lumpy.
*Possible causes:* heating the butter too much before adding the flour. Beating the sauce too little. Letting a skin form before reheating the sauce.
*Remedy:* put the sauce through a fine strainer, or liquidize in a blender. Then reheat in a clean pan, preferably a double boiler. Remember to beat liquids into sauces off the heat, and to beat the sauce continuously after returning it to the heat to thicken it. It's also a good idea to have liquids warm when adding them.
*Problem:* skin has formed on top.
*Principal cause:* letting sauce sit uncovered.
*Remedy:* one way to prevent a skin from forming is to keep back a little of the liquid to be added, and to cover the surface with this reserved liquid when the sauce has thickened. Another way is to cover the top of sauce with wet waxed paper (use cold water), pressing the wet paper over the whole surface. Sometimes a well fitting lid will serve as enough cover to prevent skinning, but this doesn't always work.
*Problem:* sauce has a raw taste.
*Principal cause:* not cooking the roux before adding the liquids.
*Remedy:* cook the sauce a little longer.
*Problem:* sauce is not glossy.
*Principal cause:* not cooking the sauce a bit longer after it has thickened.
*Remedy:* cook the sauce for at least two minutes more after it has thickened, stirring continuously or beating with a balloon whisk. This will insure that all the starch in the flour has gelatinized, which is what gives the sauce a gloss.

Below: a skin will form on a sauce only a short time after you make it if you let it sit uncovered. Try covering it closely by pressing wet wax paper over the surface.

Right: when a sauce is lumpy, you can usually save it by pressing it through a fine sieve, and reheating it in a double boiler.

*Problem:* sauce thins down when mixed with other foods.
*Possible causes:* failing to drain the foods to be sauced. Using acid foods, such as tomatoes, with the sauce.
*Remedy:* blend a little cornstarch with milk—1 tablespoon cornstarch will usually do to thicken 2 cups of thinned sauce—and beat into the sauce. Stir well while reheating. Another method is to add a small amount of *beurre manié*, stirring continuously over low heat until sauce is of the right consistency again. Always add acid foods, such as tomatoes, after the sauce has thickened, and adjust the consistency with *beurre manié.*
Note: to make *beurre-manié*—in a bowl off heat, blend equal parts of flour and butter (about 1 tablespoon of each) into a paste. A small supply of *buerre manié* can be kept on hand in a plastic bag in the refrigerator.
*Problem:* mayonnaise curdles.
*Possible causes:* adding the oil too quickly. Not beating the egg yolks sufficiently.
*Remedy:* start again with two fresh yolks. Add the curdled mayonnaise, drop by drop (it must be drop by drop) until the mixture becomes thick, opaque, and almost white. Then add the curdled mayonnaise a little faster, teaspoonfuls at a time.
*Problem:* custard sauce curdles.
*Possible causes:* heating too quickly. Failing to stir continuously. Not using a double boiler when reheating to thicken.
*Remedy:* as soon as there is any sign of curdling, strain the sauce and beat it vigorously. You can also try putting it in the blender; the blender action may break down the curd so that the sauce becomes smooth again.

# New Ways, Old Ways

# 5

Historians describe different stages in human development by the material that had the greatest significance in our progress at a particular stage. They speak, for example, of the Stone Age, the Bronze Age, the Iron Age. Perhaps some future historian, after the passing of several more millenia, will describe the age in which we are living today as the Package Age.

Practically all our foodstuff is prepackaged: in paper, plastic, foil, tin, or glass; in boxes, bags, or bottles. Most of it, too, has been processed in some way, from mere washing to precooking to full preparation as a meal. Many people are reacting against this wrapping and double wrapping, particularly those who feel that a responsibility toward the environment includes a concern about packaging materials that do not decompose as waste products—that is, are not biodegradable. Nevertheless, most modern cooks take for granted, and welcome, the great variety of convenience foods piled high on supermarket shelves. In fact, some convenience foods are cheaper than unprocessed food, and so can help the budget stretch a bit farther. The economy factor never applies to fully prepared meals, but there are savings in using canned ham, frozen juices, packaged chicken chow mein, and canned spinach, beets, peas, tomatoes, and applesauce, for example. Therefore, the wise shopper—and good cook, too—chooses some convenience foods to save time, money, and effort.

The trend, however, is toward using more and more processed and packaged foods, and today, the average American shopping basket contains more convenience foods than any other kind. European countries are also

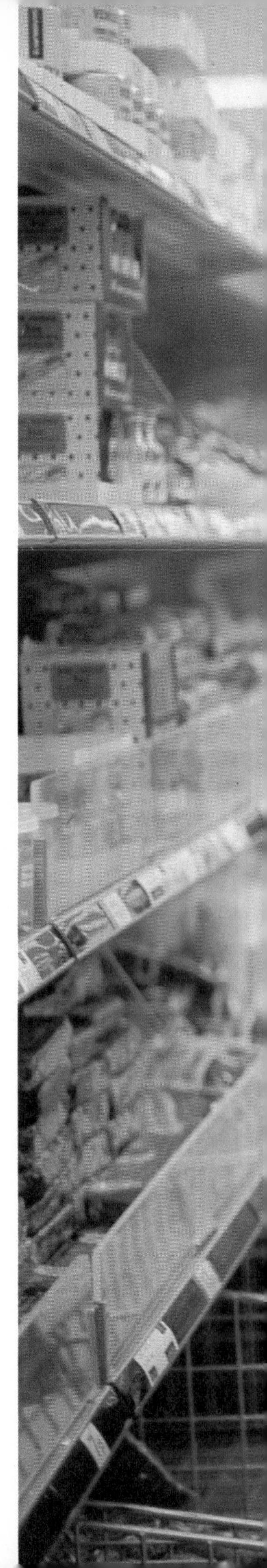

The wealth of package mixes on your supermarket shelves tempts you to take the shortcuts in cooking. Many times you'll want to do just that—but with a personal touch that adds something special.

catching up with the trend. In Great Britain, for example, about one-fourth of all food purchases are convenience foods. Marketing forecast suggests that we will be using still more convenience foods in the future. Yet, only a short while ago, many of our favorite packaged foods had not even been thought of.

The greatest change in our buying and eating habits has come in the last quarter of a century. Previous generations of cooks actually resisted convenience foods, many feeling that their vital role as food providers was threatened by the food manufacturer. To overcome this reluctance to use convenience foods, many manufacturers marketed products that required one important, though simple, operation to be carried out by the user. For instance, a cake mix had to have a beaten egg added. The psychology of this worked, and more people began to use mixes because they felt they were doing something in the actual preparation of them. Nowadays, few people think twice about using a mix. Perhaps we have become conditioned to speed and convenience. Perhaps we genuinely feel that our skills can be better used in more creative ways to insure the well-being of our families. On the other hand, there is some concern that, if we all buy the same kinds of prepared foods, we will lose all variety and originality in our meals.

Today's clever cooks have one answer to this possible problem: they add their own individual touch to any prepared food or mix. They still cook to please their own family's tastes, and they can still take pride in serving an attractively prepared and presented meal. Often no one is any the wiser about whether or not a mix was used. More important, does it really matter if it were known?

It can be fun to scout the many convenience foods available, and then to think of all the different touches you can add to them. Devise your own special treatments, and you'll be getting the best of both worlds—the convenience of having the basic preparation done, and the creativity of doing your own thing.

When it comes to working out variations on

Here are some sparkling samples of mixes plus.

Left: this pineapple upside down cake started with a yellow cake mix.

Left center: a gingerbread mix turned into this layer cake filled with mashed bananas.

Left below: a simple mix becomes a hard-to-resist layer cake filled and trimmed with gooey icing.

Right: all are from mixes, yet you'd think they were done by professionals.
Clockwise are: black forest cake, rich with chocolate and cherries; a pretty white meringue with fresh strawberries; a creamy rice pudding shaped like the fluted mold it was made in.

a theme, there is no end to the ways you can spruce up a mix. You've probably done a good many original things with mixes already, but here are some ideas that might be of interest.

Transform a plain cake mix into a colorful upside down cake by baking it on top of fruit. Pineapple is an old favorite to start with. Grease a cake pan *one size larger* than that recommended on the mix instructions. Pour three tablespoons of corn syrup into the pan, and arrange well-drained slices of canned pineapple, plus a few cherries for extra color, in a design. Prepare the cake mix according to the manufacturer's instructions, and carefully spread the mix on top of the pineapple. Bake in the usual way, and then turn it out with the pineapple prettily uppermost.

You can make a rhubarb lattice upside down cake in a similar way, but it will look more attractive if you bake it in a square pan. If the instructions call for an eight-inch round pan, use a seven-inch square one; if a nine-inch round pan is recommended, use an eight-inch square one. Prepare one pound of rhubarb by cutting off the ends, peeling off the thin outer skin, and cutting into two-inch pieces. Place corn syrup in the bottom of the cake pan as before, and arrange the rhubarb pieces in a lattice design. Make the mix as directed, and spread it on top of the rhubarb. When it has been baked and turned upside down, the cake will make a pretty picture

with its lattice of pink rhubarb—and it will taste deliciously different, too.

Along the same lines of combining cake with fruit, try baking a mix on top of sliced apple slices or applesauce. The spice that makes the apple so nice is cinnamon or nutmeg—and a few tablespoons of chopped raisins make it nicer still. A final suggestion: bake a gingerbread mix on top of well-drained canned pears, or golden plums.

Thought of combinations you might like better? Try them, of course. That's where the variations on a theme come in.

We usually think of frosting as the perfect topping for a cake, and we're probably in a bit of a rut on that score. Why not take a new path and try hot sauces with cakes? Here are a couple of quick-and-easy ideas.

Use the juice left over from a can of pineapple. Add a little grated lemon or orange rind, and thicken with cornstarch that has first been mixed with a little of the plain juice. (Allow one tablespoon of cornstarch for $1\frac{1}{2}$ to 2 cups of liquid.) Bring the mixture almost to the boil, and then stir in the blended cornstarch. Continue heating, stirring all the while, until the sauce thickens.

Apricot preserves lend themselves to another tasty hot sauce. Put the preserves through a sieve, thin down with a few teaspoons of orange juice, and heat gently before pouring on the cake.

Both these sauces go deliciously with the upside down cakes described—but they also make something special out of a plain cake. Another great topping for a simple cake is a fruit purée. Make one by lightly poaching fresh fruit of your choice in a small amount of water and sugar to taste; or buy canned or frozen fruit purées ready for use. For a homemade flavor in the latter case, add a squeeze of fresh lemon or orange juice.

For a dessert that looks and tastes extra special, bake a cake mix in a ring mold and fill the center with fruit. Again, your own preference and imagination are the only limits on go-togethers, but try these as a start—orange or lemon cake filled with fruit salad; devil's food cake with pears; coconut cake with crushed raspberries or strawberries.

Layer cakes are an old tried-and-true favorite, and using mixes simplifies making them. So, get out those layer cake pans and go to town—with yummy fillings between layers, of course. A few suggestions: cream cheese topped with black cherry preserves as the filler for white or yellow cake layers; apricot preserves sprinkled with chopped

Treats made with pancake mixes are many and varied. Here are just a few.
Far left: a pancake sandwich filled with a chicken-and-soup combination.

Left: rolled pancakes that you can conveniently prepare ahead of time.

Right: dessert cornet pancakes filled with flavored whipped cream.

Below right: tiny dessert pancakes bright and tempting with cherry pie filling between each.

walnuts and raisins with lemon or orange cake; brandy butter for chocolate layers; chopped dates and cream cheese with walnut cake; and mashed bananas with sugar or honey and lemon juice for gingerbread.

Another easy way of putting your own touch to a mix is to add a little something extra to the batter. Take a look in your kitchen cupboard, and you're sure to find just the brightener you want. For example, two or three tablespoons of chocolate chips do wonders for a white or yellow cake mix. A little ground nutmeg added to a chocolate cake, or a few finely chopped dried apricots to a walnut cake make an important difference. For an orange or lemon cake, try this: cut thin strips of lemon or orange rind, poach lightly in sugar syrup, and add to the batter. Finely chopped walnuts, almonds, or peanuts give a lift to an angel cake.

If you've wondered how to do something different with gingerbread, here's an idea. Make a crumble topping with equal quantities of flour, butter, and superfine or soft brown sugar, and add it halfway through the cooking time. Fruit cake is another hard-to-decorate item. Try coating it with warmed honey, and sprinkling onto this sticky topping a mixture of glacé fruits and chopped nuts.

Left: as easy to make as it is pretty to see—and good to eat—is this striped instant pudding dessert. Here it's vanilla, chocolate, and strawberry layers, but you can choose the colors and flavors you like.

Right: how about a sundae made with jello, fruit, and instant pudding? Sure to please.

Have you been taking full advantage of the versatility of pancake mix for light meals and desserts? Pancakes lend themselves to myriads of changeabouts. Moreover, if you make extras and freeze them, you'll always have the basis of a quick meal or dessert when needed.

Pancake sandwiches make a tasty treat for lunch, supper, or a hearty, leisurely breakfast—and you can use all kinds of leftovers in them as well. Have some chili con carne or creamed chicken left over from yesterday? Heat up, put between two large pancakes, and serve up to oohs and ahs. Cold meat or poultry is also adaptable for pancake filling. Slice or dice, heat in a can of condensed soup, and fill pancakes with the mixture. (If it's too runny for your taste, use as a sauce.) Try diced beef in tomato soup with a dash of cayenne pepper, cold ham in green pea or lentil soup, cold lamb in Scotch broth or mulligatawny soup, chicken or turkey in mushroom, cream of celery, or chicken soup.

Fish fillings are also good for pancakes. Flake a small can of tuna fish into cream of mushroom soup, or canned salmon or lobster into lobster bisque. It doesn't have to be soup either. Try crabmeat or scallops with a good cheese sauce; white fish fillets with parsley sauce; peeled prawns with sour cream. For a handy make-ahead meal, you can use any of these fillings rolled in pancakes instead of in sandwich form. To do so, make the pancake batter somewhat thinner than usual, roll up with the filling, and place in a big cake or roasting pan. Heat in a moderate (350°F) oven for about 20 minutes just before serving.

You can see that with a little imagination and practice, a package of pancake mix can turn magically into a nourishing and delicious light meal. However, pancake mix is also a good standby for dessert—in a hurry or not. Add frozen or canned fruits, or canned pie filling, and your humble pancake becomes a special dessert. To serve, pile small pancakes up with the fruit filling in between. Add a spoonful or two of fruit cordial to the filling for festive occasions. Another attractive way to serve dessert pancakes is to shape larger

ones into cornets, and pipe into them a filling of your favorite instant pudding. Eat cold.

An easy way to do family dessert pancakes —and one that is becoming more popular— is to top pancakes with a favorite sauce, such as chocolate, cranberry, caramel, blueberry, or strawberry. A small can of sweetened condensed milk blended with an egg yolk and the rind and juice of a lemon also makes a quick and tasty cold sauce for dessert pancakes. Butterscotch candy can be melted in evaporated milk and corn syrup for an easy-to-do butterscotch sauce—but this is for those who don't have to keep a watch on their waistlines.

Just for the fun of it, garnish your dessert pancakes. Crushed peanut brittle, chocolate match sticks or chocolate mints, crystallized ginger, glacé cherries, a twist of fresh orange or lime peel, or chopped nuts turn a simple dish into an elegant one—and so easily.

When you're pressed for time, instant puddings can be simply and effectively dressed up. As a first step, any dessert looks special if served in a beautiful glass dish, or turned out of a fancy mold. Then, you can fancy up the taste of a package pudding by adding a tablespoon or two of rum, brandy, Madeira, or sweet sherry. Especially good liqueur-and-pudding combinations are Tia Maria or Grand Marnier with chocolate; Curaçao or Cointreau with strawberry or raspberry; Kümmel or Crême de Menthe with coffee or caramel. Other tasty additions to instant puddings are finely chopped nuts or crystallized fruit, small pieces of marshmallow (cut these with scissors dipped in hot water), or chocolate chips. Fold any of these in the pudding after the milk has been added.

Adapt the popular striped jello dessert to instant puddings by making three puddings of different colors and layering them in a tall dessert glass. Let each layer set firmly before adding a new one, of course. This process is fairly quick with instant cold-mix puddings. Try chocolate, vanilla, and strawberry, or raspberry, banana, and orange, or any colors and flavors you like together.

Another time-saving and delicious use of instant puddings is as pie fillers in a crumb shell. You can use the puddings on their own, or pour them over a layer of fresh, frozen, or canned fruit. There are many crumb pastry recipes around, and you probably have a favorite already, but here's an easy and usually successful one: crush 1½ cups of graham crackers, gingersnaps, vanilla wafers, or zwieback. Add up to ½ cup sugar, and ½ cup melted butter or margarine. Mix well, and line a 9-inch pie plate, patting firmly with your fingers or the back of a spoon. Chill until firm in the refrigerator.

If you want a firm, crisp crust that is easier to cut, you can bake the crumb shell for 8 minutes at 375°F.

Crumb crusts keep well in an airtight metal or plastic box, so you can make a few ahead of time and keep them on hand for that moment of desperation when a quick, but rather special, dessert is called for. At that moment, whip out a tasty crumb shell, and fill it with small scoops of ice cream, or with fruit folded in whipped cream. Here again, the instant pudding teamed with fruit will make a fast, good, and attractive dessert.

One more instant pudding dessert that's a favorite with the kids combines pudding and graham crackers in a different way. A deep square or oblong glass dish is best for this. Put a layer of whole graham crackers in the dish, and pour vanilla pudding over them. Put another layer of graham crackers on top of the pudding, and pour chocolate pudding over this second layer. Crush graham crackers, and sprinkle generously over the top. It makes a pretty sight when cut, it's even easier than crumb crust, and almost everyone likes it. Of course, you can substitute any instant pudding flavors and colors you prefer.

Although most of us are content to rely heavily on convenience foods, it's fun now and again to look along the supermarket shelves—or in a health food store or delicatessen—to see basic commodities that got there with little or no help from the food processor. Food such as corn grits and cornmeal, pearl barley, oatmeal, and dried beans, lentils, black-eyed peas, and split peas are old-fashioned, hearty, versatile—and almost untouched as far as processing goes. We may have become so used to buying prepackaged meat that it's a novelty to see a butcher at work on a special cut of meat. When most people buy fish exclusively from the deep freeze counter, it can be a rare treat to see fish straight from the sea—complete with head, tail, and fins. In fact, it can be like an outing to shop in an old-time market with fresh vegetable and fruit stalls along with the other "natural" food. Many children find such shopping trips a real education, and many adults like the reminder of the "good old days".

There's another aspect to the backward look on traditional food, and that is the interesting and wide divergence of cooking styles in our United States. In any country this size, you would naturally expect to find

great differences in dishes and eating patterns in various regions. Many of these differences in American styles of cooking spring from the fact that our ancestors came from many parts of the world. Each tended to settle in an area with friends and relatives from the same home country, and to cook as they had traditionally. It would be losing a vital part of our own heritage and history if we lost sight of traditional dishes and regional specialties.

So when convenience foods began to seem drab and ordinary, search out an old cookbook and get a recipe for, say, shrimp creole, Boston baked beans and brown bread, chicken gumbo, Brunswick stew, Maryland crab cakes, New England clam chowder, or any of the biscuits, breads, quick breads, and cakes of old.

Remember when you do traditional cooking that a lot depends on look, smell, and feel. Our grandmothers and great grandmothers seldom went by the book, and when a recipe did get written down, it merely represented one woman's way of doing it. So use your judgment, experience, and own way of doing things. Taste often—and add more herbs or seasoning if you think they're light, even if the recipe clearly states $\frac{1}{4}$ teaspoon of this or that. Change seasonings, too. If you hate sage, cut the sage; if you love chervil, add a pinch. Then you'll be cooking in the traditional way—and if you care about the art of cooking, you'll enjoy acquiring the practices that have stood the test of time.

Many recipes call for stock, and a good old-fashioned stock has no equal for lending full, rich flavor to a dish. Stock requires long slow cooking, but modern pressure cooking

Right: golden brown outside, delicately yellow inside, an old-fashioned pound cake is a melt-in-the-mouth treat. Whichever of the traditional recipes you follow, take the hints shown in the photographs opposite (reading from the left to right). Cream the butter and sugar very well. Beat in egg yolks thoroughly. Beat egg whites and put aside before measuring the flour. Add part of the flour gradually. Add the egg whites before the rest of the flour. Beat all ingredients until the batter is creamy smooth.

can cut the time considerably. Even without the shorter cooking time, stock doesn't take too much attention during the long process, so you may find it's worth the effort because of the bonus in extra taste. To prepare stock the old tried-and-true way, simmer meat bones, meat trimmings, vegetables (use root vegetables because green ones will cloud the liquid), and herbs (sage and thyme are good standbys, but try others) in water to cover. Cook for three hours or more—one hour in a pressure cooker—skim off the fat that has collected on top, and strain.

While you're thinking along traditional lines, go back to those dried beans we mentioned at the beginning of this chapter. Dried beans are a good source of protein, which makes them a welcome substitute for expen-

Left: among the treasures of traditional American foods are Boston baked beans and brown bread.

Right: creole dishes—mostly from New Orleans—rank with the world's great foods. These delectable examples include shrimp and okra jumbo (in tureen), red snapper creole, and baked oysters Lafitte.

Below: many a hearty oldtime dish starts with dried beans. They are a healthy and economical addition to your diet.

sive meat. They are even more economical when you consider that they double in bulk when cooked. Most cookbooks have dried bean soup and casserole recipes, and vegetarian cookbooks abound in them. Try dried limas, kidneys, navy, soy, pinto, or black-eyed peas, among others.

Another kind of old-fashioned cooking in which there is a lot of modern interest is bread making. There is something deeply satisfying in making a batch of dough—and the satisfaction is even greater when you know that homemade bread is of greater flavor than most bakery bread. It can be almost a mystical experience for a family to sit down together and share a loaf of home baked bread. Although many people think bread making is complicated and beset with problems, it is one of the easiest kinds of baking, in reality. There is no daring attached to using yeast as a leavening agent. Yeast is simply a living plant that acts in a predictable way. For example, to grow and produce the gas needed to raise the bread, yeast needs warmth—an oven with only the pilot light on will do, or a warm spot in any room. The dough won't flop if someone slams the back door, and it doesn't go temperamental if a draft strikes it for a few minutes. Pay no attention to these and other old-wives tales, and you'll have fun in baking bread.

Briefly, here are a few tips to help you make delicious bread.

Granular yeast or yeast cakes give about the same results, so use whichever is easiest to get. Soften it so it will blend evenly. Do this by sprinkling or crumbling over lukewarm water or milk and letting it stand a few

minutes. Be sure the liquid is lukewarm; if it's hot, the yeast will be killed, and if it's cold, the yeast won't grow.

If you're in a great hurry, work with warm ingredients, and make the dough in a warm place. Otherwise, have everything at room temperature, and let the dough rise slowly. The results are better with long, slow rising.

If it's more convenient, you can make good bread by mixing the dough the night before, and leaving it to rise in the refrigerator overnight. Simply let it return to room temperature the next day, and then form into loaves.

Dough usually needs to rise twice, but recipes vary and you should check this point. When it is left to rise, it is essential that the dough is covered to prevent the surface from drying. A sheet of well-greased plastic makes

an ideal cover, or use a damp cloth. You can also leave dough to rise in a large plastic box with a tight lid. Never leave rising dough uncovered.

Use bread flour if you can get it. If not, all-purpose flour will do, but you will have to knead the dough more to get a well-risen loaf. Brown bread never rises as well as white bread, so don't expect it to. For a lighter

You can almost smell the goodness of these stick-to-your-ribs breads that you can make in your own kitchen. They're wholesome and flavorsome, and made with whole meal flours and grains. Which could become your family favorite?
Left to right: Finnish health bread, cumin-buckwheat ring, currant muffins, Swedish steamed rye log, sesame breakfast buns, buckwheat-banana biscuits, and fennel rye flat bread.

A home garden with squash, cabbage, corn, and other family favorites is a sure way of getting plenty of really fresh vegetables—and today, more and more people are growing their own. The children love to help, too.

brown loaf, mix up to half white flour in with the wholemeal flour. You can make a good brown bread with one rising. (You knead and let dough rise to improve the texture, but brown bread texture is always close, so you can take this short cut.)

For a richer dough, add shortening (butter, lard or bland cooking oil), or eggs. The richer the dough, the finer the texture of the finished bread. However, rich doughs don't rise as much because shortening and eggs make the yeast action slower.

For a shiny crust, brush the top of the risen loaf with beaten egg blended with a little water and sugar. For a crisp crust, brush the top with salt water. For a soft crust, brush the top with milk or oil.

Bread is done when it feels firm, and the bread pan sounds hollow when tapped on the bottom. The best temperature for bread is 425°F. A slightly lower temperature is often recommended for sweet or enriched breads.

One of the nicest things about baking your own bread is that an accident can have a happy ending. For example, you may discover when you've underbaked your bread that your family prefers it so, because it's moister. So set aside your worries about doing the perfect loaf of bread, and enjoy the fun of making and eating whatever comes out of your oven.

One final tip about home bread making. You'll find that warm bread just out of the oven is irresistible to all—so don't cut into a new loaf until it's cold, or you won't have a crumb left for tomorrow's breakfast!

How about growing your own vegetables? More and more people are doing it today in another modern trend toward old-fashioned living and eating. One reason is that you don't have to have a special large plot nowadays—the many new varieties of dwarf vegetables help, and also the fact that you can grow vegetables along the edge of the flower garden, in barrels and pots, on strings up the garage or carport wall.

Once growing them, how do you take best advantage of garden vegetables? For one thing, you should cook fresh vegetables lightly, and for the shortest possible time. For another, you should always try to pick some of them young. In fact, certain vegetables ought to be used young—string beans, for example. String beans should be picked frequently as they grow.

Gather fresh garden peas before their pods are tight, and use them within a few hours. This is one of the vegetables that deteriorates

rapidly in taste after a short time—and you won't believe how different peas are until you try them very soon after picking. Peas are a particularly good choice for home growing because, if you plant the early, mid-season, and late varieties all at the same time, you can eat the crops one after the other.

Zucchini should be picked as soon as its flower fades from the tip. Such young ones need neither peeling nor seeding for cooking. Nor do they need any dressing up. Just cook young zucchini lightly in a little oil in a covered pan, and sprinkle with fresh or dried herbs—perhaps basil or oregano—before serving.

Tomatoes, carrots, Brussels sprouts, spinach, cabbage—choose your favorites and grow them yourself. It's an old-fashioned touch that any modern can enjoy.

# Food with a Foreign Accent
# 6

A big part of the fun of a vacation in a foreign country is eating completely different food. Trying a new dish that you have never had at home is a happy kind of adventure, and eating the same food as the people who live in the place you're visiting helps you learn about their way of life. To sample a Scandinavian smorgasbord heaped with varieties of hot and cold seafood, meat, vegetables, poultry, eggs, and mountains of bread and butter (from which the spread gets its name), is to sense the wonderful warmth of a lengthy, hearty meal when the weather is witheringly cold outside —as it is for a large part of the year in the far north of Europe. To taste a highly spiced Mexican taco that heats up your insides is to understand the centuries-old custom in very hot countries of using spices heavily to preserve meat, and perhaps to cover up a slight spoilage.

With supersonic travel shrinking the earth, more and more Americans are able to eat the traditional foods they read about or hear about in the country of origin. However, we don't have to travel to enjoy foreign cookery, delightful as going away may be. Right here at home we can go out to restaurants featuring food from other lands, and right here in the home we can cook dishes typical of various countries the world over. Fortunately, most large towns in the USA have well-stocked stores with the ingredients needed to cook Chinese, Japanese, or Indian food, Turkish, Austrian, or Portuguese dishes, Mexican or Jamaican specialties—in fact, almost any national cuisine that takes your fancy. So let's think about the idea of sparking the family menu with that something different: a dish—or a whole meal—with a foreign accent.

A food adventure is in store for you if you try a typical dish of another country. This Japanese meal is particularly easy because each diner cooks his own food at the table.

Italian cooking can now pretty much be said to be part of the American scene. But have you ever stopped to analyze what makes an Italian dish Italian?

One thing is that cooking styles depend a great deal on natural resources. So in Italy, you will find that many dishes glow with the tomatoes that grow so abundantly there. The famous Parmesan cheese—dry, crumbly, and easy to grate—is widely used in many everyday dishes, and to sprinkle liberally on soup and pasta. Oil from the olives growing in groves in the warm sun, and the widespread garlic plant are other homegrown ingredients used constantly in Italian cooking. Italians like full flavored herbs such as sweet basil, mild and sweet marjoram, rosemary, fennel, oregano, and juniper berries. In addition, the hard wheat that thrives in the Italian climate is excellent for that all-popular pasta. Rice also flourishes in Italy; hence the many rissottos and other rice-based dishes associated with Italian cooking. (In parts of Italy, spaghetti and rice are eaten simply with a dressing of olive oil and a sprinkle of Parmesan cheese.) Italy is an important wine producing country, so its inhabitants often use wine in their cooking.

In contrast to Italian food, Greek food is less well known in the United States, but it, too, has its interesting aspects. Greek food seems designed for cooking and eating out of doors. Meat is skewered and done on an open fire or a charcoal burner—and thus are created the kabobs typical of Greece. For a

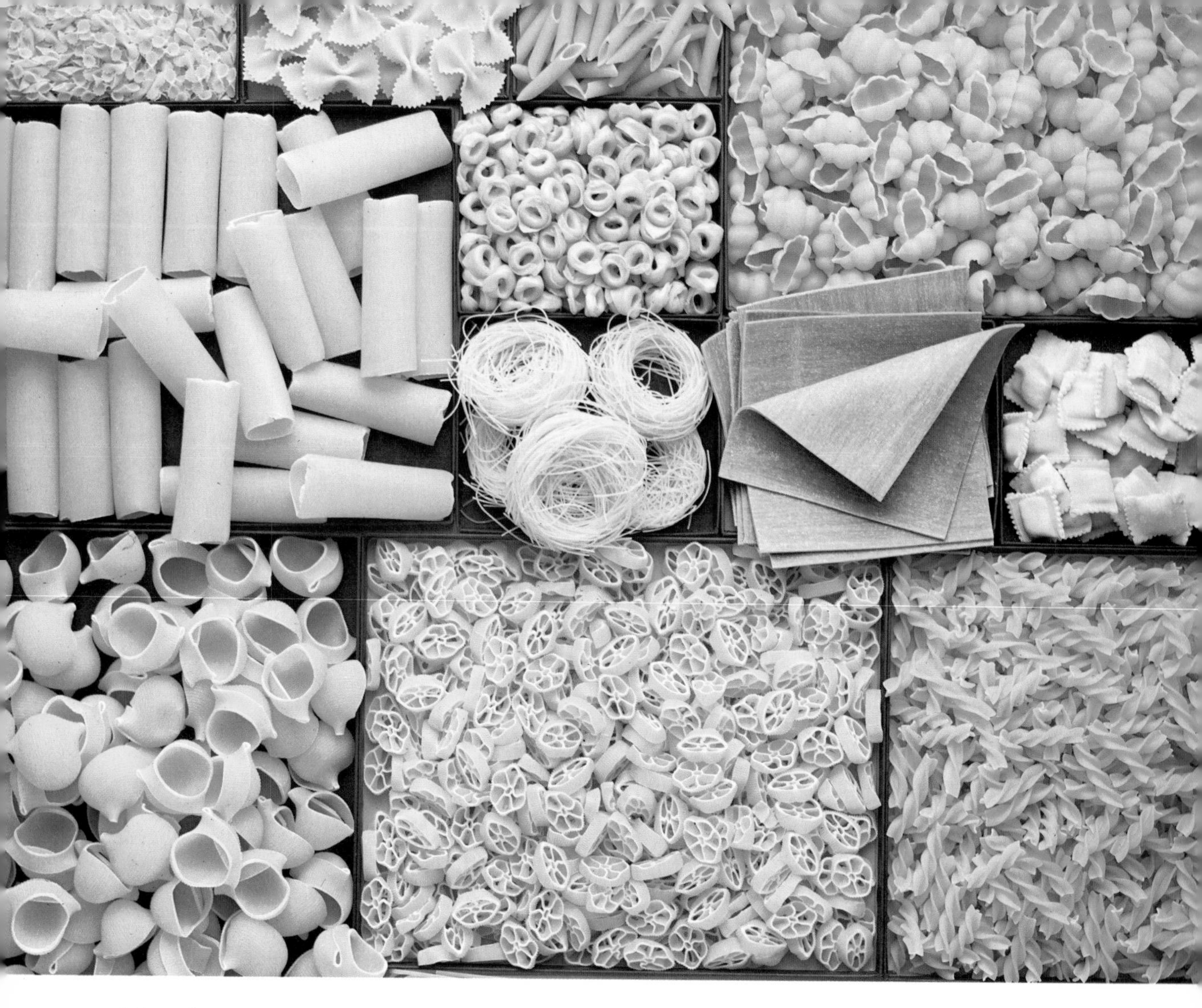

celebration meal, whole baby lamb may be roasted on a hand-turned spit over an open fire. The taste of the outdoors also springs from the use of wild herbs such as marjoram, oregano, thyme, sage, and rosemary, which grow abundantly on the wooded mountain-sides. Many wild plants, such as dandelions and charlock (wild mustard), are also collected and eaten as vegetables and salads in the height of summer, when garden plants are parched from lack of water.

Greece is not a big meat producing country, and most meat available is tough and dry. To overcome these difficulties, the Greeks have devised many recipes made with finely ground meat, enriched with seasoning and flavoring ingredients. Ground meat kabobs, squash and eggplant stuffed with ground meat, and the well-known moussaka—ground meat and eggplant baked in layers with a sauce—are all delicious dishes that disguise tough meat. The use of lemon juice in meat dishes also helps to tenderize the meat.

Many people have the mistaken idea that all French cooking is time-consuming and elaborate. They imagine that the ordinary cook stands over the stove continuously, stirring and beating, skimming and blending, using a host of expensive and fancy ingredients. In fact, some French specialties need this kind of care and involvement—navarin of lamb and pot au feu, for example. Some dishes also involve many stages, each of which is essential for the high quality of the finished dish. However, there are also numerous French recipes that are simple and easy to make. For instance, omelets, the delicious open savory tarts called "quiche", and many casseroles

Left: pasta in every size and shape—green as well as white—invites you to cook it in one of the delicious ways the Italians do.

Right: tender lamb, skewered with vegetables and grilled or broiled, gives you one of the kabobs that the Greeks are famous for.

are no more difficult to prepare than many of our own favorite dishes—yet they will have an unmistakable French quality.

The typical French flavor derives from a combination of herbs, garlic, and wines that are used together in many dishes. In France, most country houses have their own herb gardens, and herbs are carefully gathered and dried for use throughout the winter. Among the most commonly used herbs are parsley, thyme, tarragon, chives, chervil, bay leaf, basil, and fennel. Often a *bouquet garni*, containing a combination of three or more of these herbs, is used in stews, casseroles, and soups. The *bouquet garni* is a small bag filled commonly with parsley, thyme, and bay leaf, but it can have other herbs called for in a given recipe. You can make your own from a square of thin, soft material such as muslin, lawn, or cheesecloth. Simply tie the corners together after placing the herbs on the cloth, or tie the herbs in the cloth with some string. Remember to take the *bouquet garni* out before the dish is served. You don't want to have someone get a soggy, discolored bit of unchewable fabric in their food.

France is a leading wine producing country, so wine is always available for cooking. The French choose a young wine, which is cheaper than an aged wine, but one of good quality always. Don't make the mistake of using an inferior wine in French recipes. If the wine used is too fruity or too vinegary, the finished dish will retain these flavors instead of the full fragrance it will have when made with a good wine.

Although we often get the impression that French cooking is rich and extravagant, the French cook is extremely thrifty in reality. For example, she uses many ingredients we might scorn to buy—bones for stock, oxtail for soups and stews, pig's head, calve's feet, bacon rinds, to name some. The good French homemaker never wastes food, and can concoct delicious dishes, such as the quiche mentioned before, from humble leftovers.

Cooking the French way doesn't involve any techniques that you probably don't know already. It's loving attention, care, and skill in putting those techniques to use that distinguishes French cooking. Let's take the making of a pâté, which you may think only a chef in an exclusive French restaurant can tackle. You, too, can make a pâté, just like most French homemakers do. In fact, with a little practice, you can develop your own recipe—and it will be called *pâté maison*, to show that it originated in your own home.

To make a pâté, you can use any kind of baking ware, preferably of glazed pottery, porcelain, enamelled iron, or ovenproof glass. There is a special mold called a *terrine* that's perfect for pâté, but a casserole, soufflé dish, or even a bread pan will do, if you can fit it with a lid.

The ingredients include meat, wine, spices, seasonings such as shallots and garlic, and pork fat. The meat will usually be ground pork and veal, and sometimes liver, plus cubes of other meats, poultry, or liver. Cognac is the most often used wine, but it could be port or Madeira as well. Spices, of course, vary. Fresh pork fat is a must for pâté; it lightens the texture of the meat mixture, and prevents it from getting dry. You can use fat back or fat trimmed from fresh leg or loin of pork. In a pinch, you can even use salt pork or thick strips of fatty bacon simmered for 10 minutes in water to desalt them.

In the process of making pâté, you line whatever dish you're using completely with pork fat. Then comes half of the mixed meats, spices, and seasoning, then a layer of cubed meat, poultry, or liver, then the rest of the meat mixture. On top you'll put more pork fat all over, and then a snug cover of aluminum foil. Put the lid on the dish, and place it in a pan deep enough to fill with water halfway up the sides of the pâté container. Bake in a moderate (350°) oven for two hours, keeping in mind that a long loaf shape will get done faster than a round or oval one.

After cooking, the pâté must be weighed down on top while it cools to room temperature. Use a sturdy block of wood, part of a meat grinder, or a heavy pot or casserole. Finally, chill the pâté, still with the weight in place. Then comes the wonderful moment when you serve it—smooth, tasty, different, and satisfying either as an appetizer, or as a light meal with French bread and salad.

Strangely enough, Chinese cooking has quite a lot in common with French cooking. In both of them, great attention is paid to the right choice of flavoring ingredients, such as spices and herbs. In both, too, most dishes have a wide variety of ingredients, a good stock or dry wine is used to moisten the food, and mushrooms, onions, and garlic are much esteemed and generally used.

What makes the flavor of Chinese food different are ingredients not normally used in Western cooking. These include soy sauce, chili sauce, young root ginger, hoisin sauce, and five-spice powder, which is a blend of star anise, anise pepper, fennel, cloves, and cinnamon. Other distinctive flavorings come from spicy shrimp sauce, thick oyster sauce, and sweetish plum sauce.

You don't need all the rare spices of the Orient in order to cook Chinese food in your own home, though. The basic materials are much the same as Western ones, and nowadays soy sauce is sold as a common condiment in most supermarkets. You can also use acceptable substitutions for Chinese in-

gredients that are impossible or difficult to purchase. For example, tabasco is a good substitute for chili sauce, chutney for plum sauce, salted sauerkraut for pickled cabbage, capers for black beans, carrot for bamboo shoots, and cinnamon for star anise. Dry sherry will do well in the place of Chinese wines, which are seldom obtainable. Be careful when it comes to using anything else but root ginger, however. Ground ginger, which seems to be a natural, just won't do. Better to wash all the syrup off crystallized ginger and slice that, or use coarsely grated lemon rind.

Another particular characteristic of Chinese cooking is that practically all ingredients are cut into bite-size pieces before being cooked. Meat, poultry, fish, vegetables, and other components are sliced wafer thin, or cut into matchstick strips, or small dice not more than half an inch long.

One of the most typical seasonings of the noted French cuisine is a *bouquet garni,* composed of parsley, thyme, and bay leaf. It can be used loose or in a muslin bag.

A great deal of Chinese food is cooked by a quick method called "stir-frying" or, sometimes, "quick-frying". In stir-frying, a little oil is first heated in a round-bottomed utensil called a "wok". The Chinese prefer to use an oil that will add no flavor of its own to the food, such as peanut oil. When the oil is hot, a small amount of chopped onion and an even smaller amount of garlic or ginger, or both, are cooked together for a short time. Then, if the dish has both meat and vegetables, the meat is added and stirred briskly and constantly for a minute or two over high heat. It is then removed, the vegetables are added, and the seasoning is adjusted. The meat is then returned to the pan, and stir-fried for a couple more minutes together with the vegetables. At this point, a little broth and wine are usually added. This not only prevents burning, but also produces a sauce. If desired, the sauce is thickened with two or three teaspoons of cornstarch.

To get an idea how quick and easy a stir-fried meat dish can be, let's look at how you would make beef strips with onion. You would start by rubbing salt, sugar, pepper, and cornstarch into beef that has been cut into matchstick strips, and marinate the meat in a mixture of sherry and soy sauce for 15 minutes. Meanwhile, make a broth of a chicken stock cube, water, sherry, and cornstarch, to be ready when you need it. In your ordinary skillet or a shallow pan, you would then stir-fry thinly sliced onion and ginger root in hot vegetable oil, followed by the beef in its marinade for $1\frac{1}{2}$ minutes. The onions are then returned to the pan and stir-fried with the meat for 30 seconds. The broth is added and all stir-fried for another 15 seconds—and the dish is served immediately.

Now you might have taken some of the mystery out of Chinese cooking, but none of the taste treat!

If you were to serve a dinner like the

typical Chinese family meal, you would have three or four dishes (of which the beef and onions could be one), rice, and soup. The soup is not eaten at the beginning of the meal, but is sipped all the way through it as a kind of beverage rather than a first course. In fact, the Chinese meal is not served in individual courses as we are used to having them, but all dishes are served together. A typical selection of dishes would be one based on meat, a second on poultry or fish, a third on eggs, and a fourth on vegetables.

Careful selection of colors, textures, and flavors is the essence of the perfect Chinese meal. For example, the cook will consider that a dry dish should be served with a juicy one, that a crunchy vegetable should accompany a soft one. Color is important, too, so white fish or nearly white poultry will be served with a yellow egg dish, or a pink sea-

Chinese food seems to be one that everyone likes at first taste. To try your hand at it, these are some of the ingredients needed.

1 Soy sauce
2 Oyster sauce
3 Chili sauce
4 Five-spice powder
5 Monosodium glutamate
6 Star anise spice
7 Plum sauce
8 Hoisin sauce
9 Bean curd
10 Water chestnuts
11 Bean sprouts
12 Black beans
13 Ginger root
14 Dried mushrooms
15 Noodles
16 Lotus root
17 Bamboo shoots
18 Pickled cabbage
19 Rice
20 Chinese cabbage

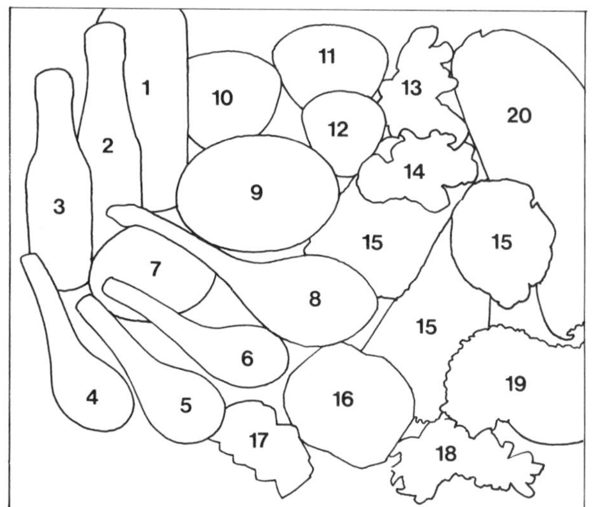

food dish, or a dish of green vegetables.

At a banquet or party, numerous dishes are served—as many as 30 different ones, and certainly not less than 10. On such occasions, the dishes are served one after the other rather than all at once, and rice comes only at the end to help settle the stomach. The Chinese seldom eat dessert after a meal, except, perhaps, at a banquet. They usually take their sweet dishes as snacks with tea.

Most people know something about Japan as a country, but comparatively few seem to know much about Japanese food. Perhaps you have been put off by learning that the Japanese eat raw fish and seafood, or hearing that the food is plain, bitty, and unfilling. You are in for a surprise if you take a closer look at Japanese cooking—and a treat if you try some of the delightful dishes.

You have already seen the kinship between great Chinese and French cooking, in which the aim is to seek the perfect blend of many various ingredients and flavorings. The Japanese aim for just the opposite in cooking: they seek to preserve separately the taste, color, and texture of each ingredient served. It is this attention to appearance as well as to taste that results in such careful and beautiful presenta-

tion, both as to arrangement of food on a plate, and of the various plates of food in a meal. The common saying about a Japanese meal is that it must be a feast for the eye and the mind as well as for the palate.

The desire for preserving the intrinsic taste of each food also means that the Japanese seldom use strong flavorings in the actual cooking process. They leave it to the individual diner to add such strong garnishes as ginger, onion, and peppery spices to the food as it is eaten. In this way, the light and subtle flavors are not overwhelmed or permeated by the heavy and strong flavors.

This exquisitely arranged setting shows how a Japanese meal is a feast for the eye as well as the palate. The dish being served is a Japanese favorite—*sashimi* (raw fish).

Like the Chinese, the Japanese use a great deal of soy sauce, but the Japanese variety is lighter and different in taste. In fact, you should use only the Japanese soy sauce if you want to get the right flavor in any Japanese food you cook.

Some of the Japanese flavoring ingredients are totally unfamiliar to the Western cook, and unique even to Oriental cooking. Among the most characteristic and unusual are soybean paste, dried kelp, dried bonito, a giant white radish tasting similar to white turnip, mild and sweet rice vinegar, and green horseradish. The dried bonito and kelp are the basis of the main stock used for soup and braising liquid.

There are many one-dish meals based on rice or noodles, but a typical Japanese main meal will have several courses. Again like the Chinese style of eating, the Japanese style of eating is to serve all the courses at one time, and to end the meal with plain rice. The Japanese, however, eat pickled vegetables with their final bowl of rice, and these pickled vegetables are another unique feature of the cuisine. Every conceivable type of vegetable is used, and different parts of the country all have their regional specialties.

As for cooking techniques, Japanese methods are very like the ways of cooking you already know. The differences could only be called variations. In broiling fish, for example, the skin is always left on, and the fish is never filleted. It is cut into small pieces, salted and left to sit for about 25 minutes, then broiled skin side up first. The layer of fat just under the skin reacts with the salt and heat, and you'll get the juiciest, tenderest piece of broiled fish you can imagine.

The Japanese are masters of deep frying, and no fried dish is ever heavy or greasy. The most famous deep fried dish is *tempura*, and it is something that you can make for your family without buying anything unusual in the way of ingredients or utensils.

Tempura should feature at least six ingredients—a mixture of meat or seafood and vegetables. (A tempura feast can have 14 different components.) The usual choices are shrimp, chicken, or pork, and several vegetables from among eggplant, green pepper, mushroom, sweet potato, spring onion, or carrot. Canned gingko nuts, bamboo shoots, or lotus root are also included. All are cut into small slices, cubes, or strips.

Japanese cooks pay special attention to the frying oil, preferring a blend of two or more to a single one—and each cook seems to have a favorite blend. You can safely use peanut, corn, or cottonseed oil on their own, but olive or sesame oils should be used only with, and in a smaller proportion to, one of the vegetable oils. Put the oil in any large pot to a depth of three inches, and heat it until it is very hot (375° on a fat thermometer).

The batter for tempura is very thin, and must be icy cold. It is made with eggs, flour, and ice water, and it is well to keep this batter cold throughout the period of use by putting it in a bowl set in ice cubes. The coldness of the batter means that, when the coated food meets the hot oil, the batter will puff and swell so that the food is partly cooked by steam inside the shell. The thinness of the batter allows the colors of the food to show through.

The Japanese don't serve desserts after a meal, although it has become a recent custom to end a dinner with fresh fruit. Tiny cakes—so complicated to make that they are left to the professionals—are only served between meals, or at the traditional tea ceremony.

Because food is eaten with chopsticks, as in China, it is always cut into small pieces before cooking, and the cooking time for most foods is short. It is customary to cook certain dishes right at the table, both in the home and at a restaurant. Usually one person does the cooking, and passes the food to each diner as it gets done, but there are several dishes that diners cook themselves in a constantly heated pot in the center of the table.

A word about Japanese tea. The most popular variety is green tea—that is, tea leaves which have been dried but not fermented. It is light and delicate in flavor, and is always drunk without sugar or lemon.

Our culinary excursion into the food of other nations has dealt with general techniques rather than exact recipes. That now leaves you all the fun of going on a cookbook tour of the world, and choosing new dishes you and your family can enjoy at your own dining table—soon.

Japan's triumphant contribution to the famous dishes of the world is *tempura,* which consists of deep-fried seafood or meat and vegetables in a thin batter (top right).

# Tips and Hints & Glossary

Think of the best cooks you know, and you'll probably notice that they have an easy air of confidence about all they do in the kitchen. They never seem to get flustered when they try something entirely new to them, and they are bold about trying experiments on their old favorites. You may say that their skill comes from a natural gift for, or love of, cooking; and it's true that liking to cook always helps. But there's more to it than that. Like any activity that takes practice and experience as well as interest and attention—from playing a good game of tennis, to making a well-fitting suit, to painting a picture—cooking skills are built on a solid foundation of knowledge. The hopeful thing about it is that it's easy, and often fun, to learn more and more about cooking. This applies whether you're just starting to cook for the first time, or whether you've been at it for a good while already.

This last section of the book is designed to add to your present store of knowledge about various foods, techniques of cooking, and culinary terms. The first part offers helpful tips and hints about meat, fish, fruits and vegetables, eggs, and cheese. In it you'll find ideas and suggestions on serving, storing, and preparing these foods, in addition to freezing them and others. In fact, there is special information on making the best use of your freezer—from which foods will or won't freeze well, to how to cut down on the running costs of this convenient appliance.

If, as most of us do, you sometimes have a moment's pause over the difference between blending, stirring, or folding in, or over directions that say sauté as opposed to fry, the glossary in the second part of this section will be most useful. It has been compiled with an eye to completeness as far as methods and techniques of cooking go, and also contains some general definitions, descriptive terms, and explanations. As a final help to you in your cooking adventures, there is a listing and description of some of the main ingredients used in Chinese and Japanese cooking, with their names given in the original languages.

The creative cook at work. With fresh, raw ingredients in hand, she'll use her knowledge, technique, and personal touch to make something special of any dish she serves.

# Meat

☐ Remove wrapping paper from meat, and store it covered in a nonairtight container in the refrigerator. A pottery casserole is ideal. Don't use sealed plastic boxes for storing meat.
☐ Uncovered meat will dry out even in the refrigerator, and the dried surfaces will be tough and tasteless when the meat has been cooked.
☐ Keep meat well wrapped in the freezer to prevent drying out. Freezer "burn" means that the meat has been completely dehydrated; it will be unappetizing when cooked.
☐ Allow large pieces of meat to defrost thoroughly and slowly before cooking. The bottom of the refrigerator is the best spot. Slow thawing reduces dripping, and keeps the meat flavorsome and juicy. Large roasts and poultry may take from 12 to 48 hours to defrost.
☐ You can cook steak and chops straight from the freezer, provided they are not too thick. However, allow all poultry—including cut up chicken—to defrost before cooking, or it will be tough.
☐ If you're in a great hurry, you can speed up the defrosting process by placing the frozen meat or poultry in its plastic wrapping in cold running water. Some flavor will inevitably be washed out, of course.
☐ Marinades containing lemon juice, vinegar, or wine help to tenderize meat as well as adding flavor.
☐ Beating or pounding meat also helps to tenderize it.
☐ If in any doubt about the toughness of a piece of meat, pot roast or braise rather than oven roast or broil. Always play safe rather than sorry when it comes to cooking meat.
☐ Sear steaks and chops under the hot broiler first. This not only gives a crisp outside, but also cuts down on loss of meat juices. Reduce heat and continue to cook more gently if you like your steaks or chops medium or well done.
☐ Browning meat for pot roasts or stews helps to seal the outside of the meat, retaining the juiciness of the meat during its subsequent cooking.
☐ Generally speaking, the higher the fat content of meat, the shorter its freezer life or storage time. The meat does not go bad, but its flavor begins to deteriorate. Keep bacon in the freezer for no more than three months, and for less time if it is smoked. Pork should be stored only for between four and six months, lamb for six to eight months, and beef for up to nine months. Ground meats and variety meats should be eaten within three months of freezing.
☐ For cooked meat dishes, storage time depends not only on fat content, but also on the amount of seasonings and flavorings used. Meat loaves, pâtés, sausages, and pot pies should not be kept longer than three months.
☐ If your meat gravy seems thin and lacking in flavor, add a packet of gelatine, previously softened in cold water. Stir until the gelatine dissolves well.

# *Fish*

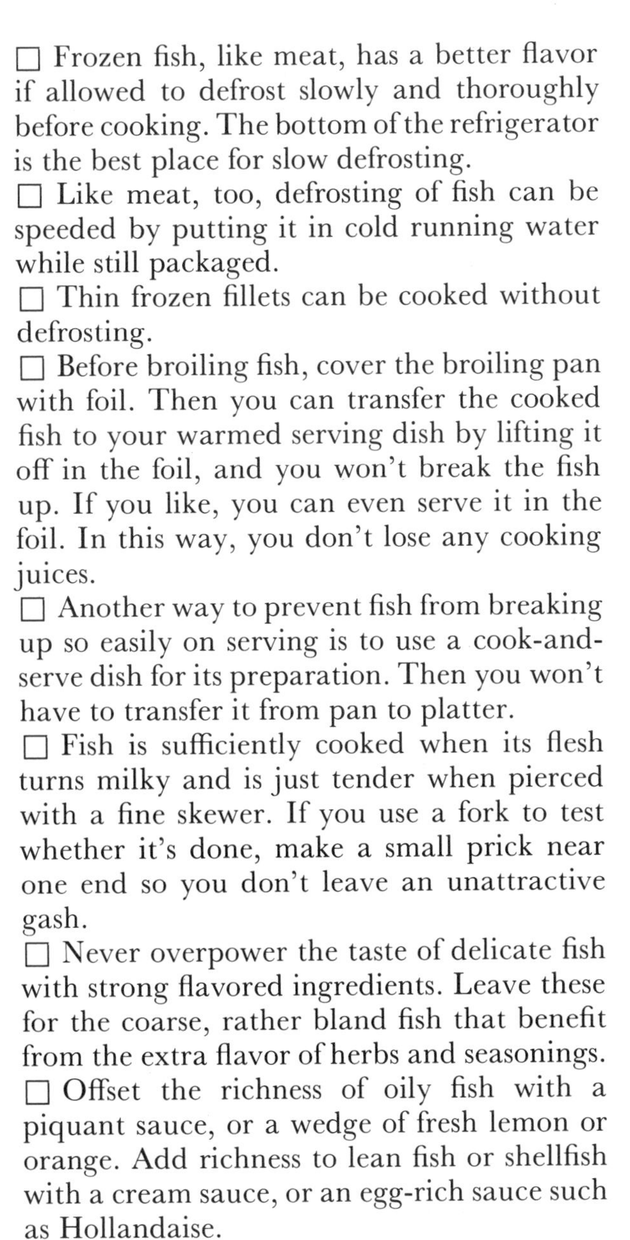

□ Frozen fish, like meat, has a better flavor if allowed to defrost slowly and thoroughly before cooking. The bottom of the refrigerator is the best place for slow defrosting.

□ Like meat, too, defrosting of fish can be speeded by putting it in cold running water while still packaged.

□ Thin frozen fillets can be cooked without defrosting.

□ Before broiling fish, cover the broiling pan with foil. Then you can transfer the cooked fish to your warmed serving dish by lifting it off in the foil, and you won't break the fish up. If you like, you can even serve it in the foil. In this way, you don't lose any cooking juices.

□ Another way to prevent fish from breaking up so easily on serving is to use a cook-and-serve dish for its preparation. Then you won't have to transfer it from pan to platter.

□ Fish is sufficiently cooked when its flesh turns milky and is just tender when pierced with a fine skewer. If you use a fork to test whether it's done, make a small prick near one end so you don't leave an unattractive gash.

□ Never overpower the taste of delicate fish with strong flavored ingredients. Leave these for the coarse, rather bland fish that benefit from the extra flavor of herbs and seasonings.

□ Offset the richness of oily fish with a piquant sauce, or a wedge of fresh lemon or orange. Add richness to lean fish or shellfish with a cream sauce, or an egg-rich sauce such as Hollandaise.

□ Shellfish such as clams, mussels, or oysters, should be bought still alive. To test if they are, tap the shell; it should close tight instantly. Discard any shells that stay open, because the organism is probably dead. Lobster and crab are also usually bought live, but can be obtained ready cooked.

□ When you're skinning fish, a little coarse dry salt sprinkled onto the skin helps you hold on to it when removing it. Rub coarse salt onto the black discoloration inside the abdomen. The coarse crystals help both to rub away the discoloration and to clean the fish.

□ Poaching small fish in vinegar helps to soften the tiny bones that are difficult to separate.

□ Some oily fish have a smell that tends to linger. Always rinse knives, plates, boards, and other utensils with cold water immediately after use with oily fish. Hot water encourages the smell to stay. If your hands retain the fishy smell, rub a little dry mustard on them, and then rinse with cold water.

□ Solid frozen juice in a package of frozen fish shows that it has not been kept at proper low temperature storage. Don't buy such a package.

□ Remember that really fresh fish has little or no "fishy smell".

# Vegetables and Fruit

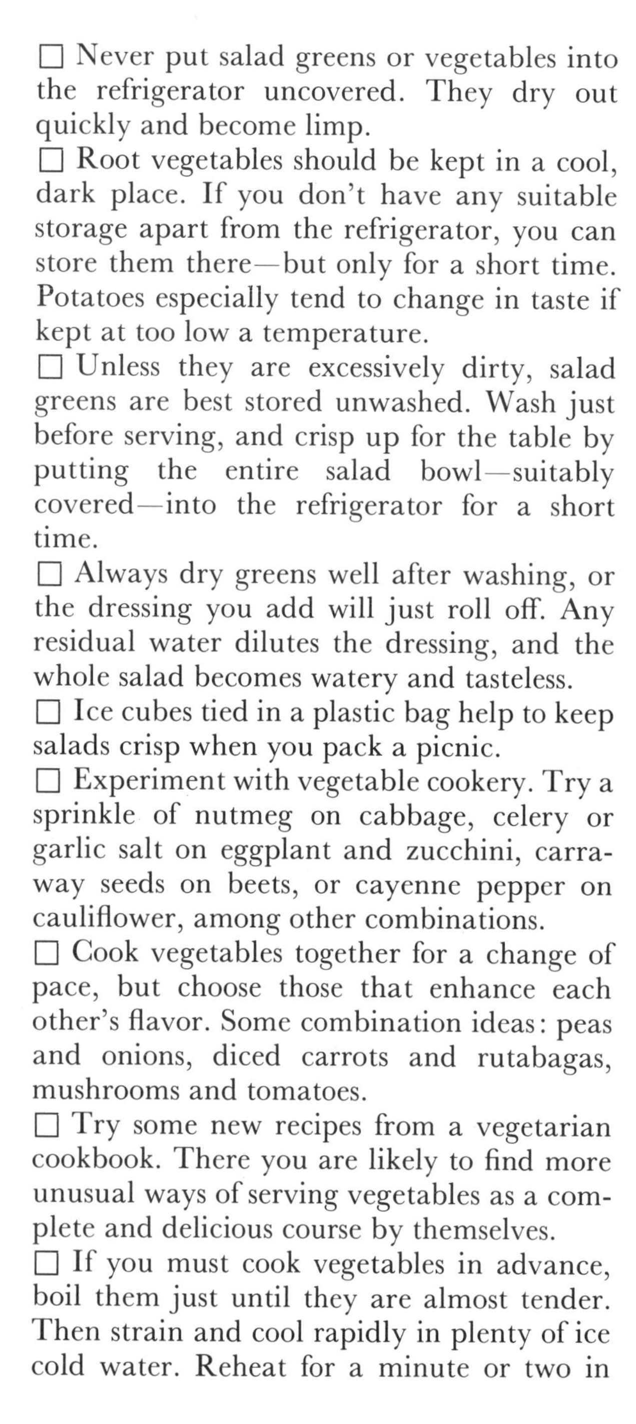

☐ Never put salad greens or vegetables into the refrigerator uncovered. They dry out quickly and become limp.
☐ Root vegetables should be kept in a cool, dark place. If you don't have any suitable storage apart from the refrigerator, you can store them there—but only for a short time. Potatoes especially tend to change in taste if kept at too low a temperature.
☐ Unless they are excessively dirty, salad greens are best stored unwashed. Wash just before serving, and crisp up for the table by putting the entire salad bowl—suitably covered—into the refrigerator for a short time.
☐ Always dry greens well after washing, or the dressing you add will just roll off. Any residual water dilutes the dressing, and the whole salad becomes watery and tasteless.
☐ Ice cubes tied in a plastic bag help to keep salads crisp when you pack a picnic.
☐ Experiment with vegetable cookery. Try a sprinkle of nutmeg on cabbage, celery or garlic salt on eggplant and zucchini, carraway seeds on beets, or cayenne pepper on cauliflower, among other combinations.
☐ Cook vegetables together for a change of pace, but choose those that enhance each other's flavor. Some combination ideas: peas and onions, diced carrots and rutabagas, mushrooms and tomatoes.
☐ Try some new recipes from a vegetarian cookbook. There you are likely to find more unusual ways of serving vegetables as a complete and delicious course by themselves.
☐ If you must cook vegetables in advance, boil them just until they are almost tender. Then strain and cool rapidly in plenty of ice cold water. Reheat for a minute or two in rapidly boiling water just before serving.
☐ French fries can be prepared in advance by cooking until they are soft but not brown. Then drain well in the deep fry basket, and plunge into very hot fat to brown just before serving. You can follow this procedure when cooking for large numbers, so you don't have to keep large quantities hot while you're frying the next batch.
☐ When you want to have vegetables in their serving dishes before you sit down to the first course at a dinner party, slightly undercook the vegetables, and place them in ovenproof dishes with a generous knob of butter. They will continue to cook in the butter, and be ready when you and your guests are.
☐ Lemon juice helps stop the browning of apples, bananas, pears, and similar fruits. When you're preparing a fruit salad, cut the fruit into a small bowl of lemon juice, and toss lightly to coat all cut surfaces. Add the lemon juice to the fruit salad syrup if you like.
☐ The top fruit of a salad prepared well in advance might begin to brown because the syrup doesn't cover it. To avoid this, cover the entire top of the salad with thin slices of lemon.
☐ A squeeze of lemon juice in the cooking water prevents new potatoes from darkening as they cook.

# Eggs

□ For boiled, poached, fried and shirred eggs, the fresher they are, the better they look and taste.

□ Very fresh eggs don't tend to break up when they are poached. Stale eggs lose their firm layer of white around the yolk. Therefore, the white becomes runny and almost impossible to keep together during poaching.

□ As an extra precaution against poached egg spread, add a little vinegar or salt to the cooking water. Both of these speed up the rate at which the egg sets.

□ Stale egg whites beat better than fresh egg whites.

□ For all baking, eggs should be at room temperature. If you plan to have a baking session in the morning, take the eggs from the refrigerator the night before.

□ Eggs beat better and more quickly when at room temperature than when cold.

□ For lighter sponge cakes, soufflés, and mousses, try beating the egg yolks over a pan of gently simmering water.

□ A little sugar added to stiffly beaten egg whites helps prevent the foam from collapsing when, for example, you're folding the whites into a mixture. Don't add the sugar too soon, however, or it will delay the foaming of the whites. In a recipe that already calls for sugar, add one tablespoon less at the beginning of the recipe, and two tablespoons of confectioner's sugar in the stiff whites at the end.

□ In a nonsweet recipe requiring stiffly beaten egg whites, a pinch of cream of tartar, or a little lemon juice, helps to keep up the volume of the foam.

□ Beat egg whites in a bowl, and make sure the beater or whisk is completely free of fat or grease. Even a trace can prevent the eggs from getting stiff. Wash all utensils immediately before use with hot soapy water, and dry with a perfectly clean towel.

□ Too much sugar added to egg yolks can delay their foaming. If a recipe requires a high proportion of sugar to eggs—as in Bavarian or Spanish creams—use only half the quantity of sugar to mix with the yolks. Add the remainder after the eggs have become thick and creamy.

□ When making an egg custard, cheat a little and beat a teaspoon of cornstarch in with the eggs and sugar. The starch raises the temperature at which thickening takes place. In other words, it is another precaution against curdling.

□ Plunge hardboiled eggs into cold running water as soon as they are done. This prevents the development of a greenish black stain around the yolk.

□ Never put a meringue onto a cold pie, because the cold causes the meringue to fall. Add the meringue when the pie is warm.

□ Raw eggs, shelled and lightly beaten with either salt or sugar, freeze well. (Label which is salt and which is sugar carefully.) Unshelled eggs will crack. Never freeze hardboiled eggs, either by themselves or in sandwiches; they become as tough as leather.

# Cheese

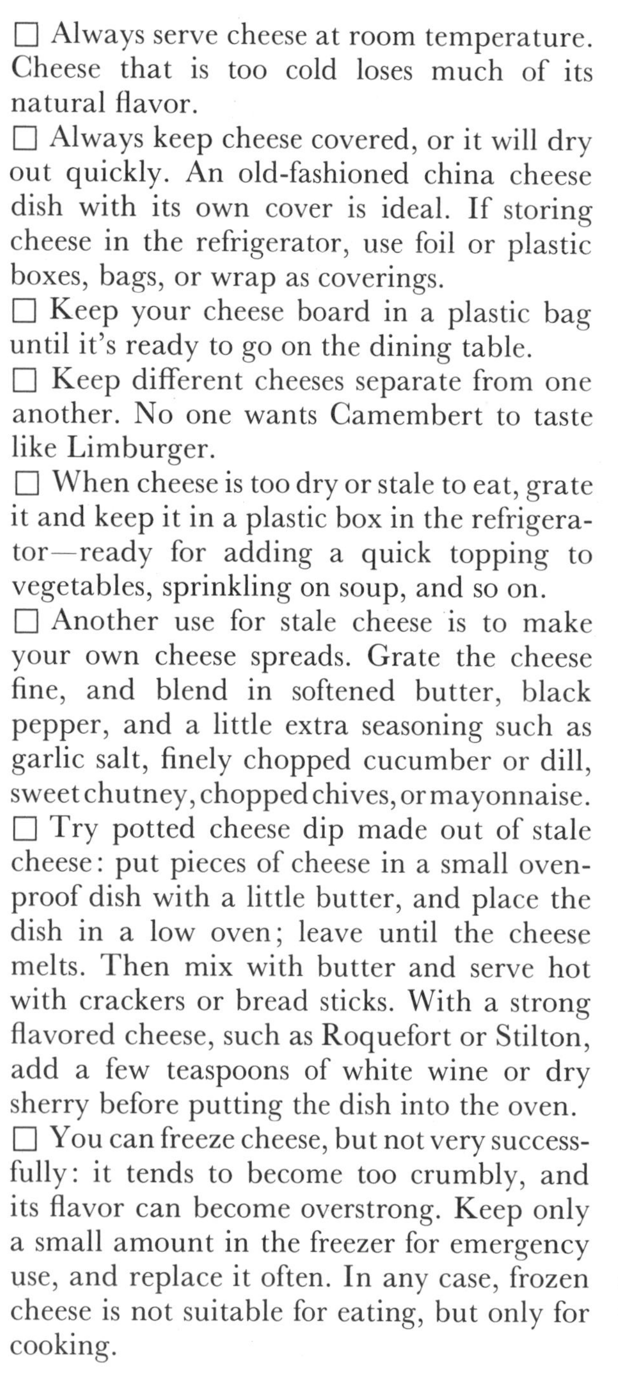

☐ Always serve cheese at room temperature. Cheese that is too cold loses much of its natural flavor.
☐ Always keep cheese covered, or it will dry out quickly. An old-fashioned china cheese dish with its own cover is ideal. If storing cheese in the refrigerator, use foil or plastic boxes, bags, or wrap as coverings.
☐ Keep your cheese board in a plastic bag until it's ready to go on the dining table.
☐ Keep different cheeses separate from one another. No one wants Camembert to taste like Limburger.
☐ When cheese is too dry or stale to eat, grate it and keep it in a plastic box in the refrigerator—ready for adding a quick topping to vegetables, sprinkling on soup, and so on.
☐ Another use for stale cheese is to make your own cheese spreads. Grate the cheese fine, and blend in softened butter, black pepper, and a little extra seasoning such as garlic salt, finely chopped cucumber or dill, sweet chutney, chopped chives, or mayonnaise.
☐ Try potted cheese dip made out of stale cheese: put pieces of cheese in a small ovenproof dish with a little butter, and place the dish in a low oven; leave until the cheese melts. Then mix with butter and serve hot with crackers or bread sticks. With a strong flavored cheese, such as Roquefort or Stilton, add a few teaspoons of white wine or dry sherry before putting the dish into the oven.
☐ You can freeze cheese, but not very successfully: it tends to become too crumbly, and its flavor can become overstrong. Keep only a small amount in the freezer for emergency use, and replace it often. In any case, frozen cheese is not suitable for eating, but only for cooking.

☐ Hard cheeses keep well, provided they are kept cool and free from mold. Soft cheeses don't keep, and should be bought ready for eating. A ripe Camembert, for example, is at its best for only a few hours. So buy it to eat the same day.
☐ For a different taste—and fewer calories—serve a slice of cheese with apple pie instead of ice cream or whipped cream. Cheddar is traditional, but milder Edam, Gouda, or Muenster are delicious, too.
☐ Give a snack meal of soup extra food value by sprinkling a generous spoonful of grated cheese on top of it.
☐ Mix an equal quantity of grated cheese and crushed cracker crumbs or crushed potato chips to make a quick gratin topping for vegetables.
☐ Cottage cheese is an ideal food for the dieter. It is very low in calories, yet rich in protein, and has little carbohydrate. Cream cheese, by contrast, is high in calories—230 calories per ounce—and has little protein. Its high calorie content is derived from the large quantity of fat it contains.
☐ The mold that grows on cheese from time to time in the best regulated household is not at all harmful. Simply trim it away with a sharp knife. Discard the moldy pieces; they will not have spoiled the flavor of the rest of the cheese.

# Freezing Foods

☐ Some vegetables, notably spinach and new carrots, can be frozen without first blanching them. Others, such as peas and beans, can be frozen for a short time—up to two months—without suffering any loss of color or flavor from lack of blanching. However, most vegetables are improved by first blanching them to stop enzyme activity before freezing them. Brussels sprouts in particular need blanching.

☐ Often fruits come onto the market at the time of year when the hot weather discourages preserving or canning. Therefore, high pectin fruits—such as lemons, oranges, different varieties of plums, blackcurrants, and gooseberries—can be frozen and made into jam later in the season. Low pectin fruits, including strawberries and raspberries, seem to lose even more of their pectin with freezing. However, you can still freeze them for later use in jam if, at the time of preserving, you add proportionately more pectin to the boiling fruit and sugar mixture.

☐ You can refreeze frozen foods provided they are still very cold, even though already soft. They will lose more flavor, of course, but they need not be discarded. Likewise, there is no reason why you should not use already frozen pastry or meat in dishes you intend to freeze anyway.

☐ Make bags for blanching vegetables before freezing from old tights cut off at the knee and thoroughly washed. Nylon net is also suitable for making blanching bags.

☐ When you are planning a big freezing session of vegetables, place plastic bowls, filled with water, in the freezer before you start. This will insure a plentiful supply of ice for rapid cooling after blanching.

☐ Pipe rosettes of whipped cream onto waxed paper. Freeze the rosettes—and you always have a good supply ready for decorating cakes, pies, and so on.

☐ Most foods freeze extremely well, but here are a few everyday ones that don't—hard-boiled eggs, bananas, light cream, and mayonnaise.

☐ If you pack lunches regularly, make sandwiches by the loaf. Separate individual sandwiches within the load with waxed paper, saran, or foil, and take out only the quantity you need at any one time.

☐ Remember to underseason dishes for freezing. Spices, herbs, and pepper tend to increase their intensity of flavor during freezing. If the food is still underseasoned upon use, you can always add extra seasoning when you reheat it. If a recipe calls for wine, don't put it in at the prefreezing stage; add it during the reheating.

☐ Cut down on running costs when your freezer is less than half full by filling the empty space with clean blankets or pillows. If you have advance notice of a power failure, pack the freezer with blankets to help keep it insulated.

☐ Before defrosting the freezer, chill several blankets in it overnight. Then use the cold blankets to wrap any still frozen food during the defrosting period.

# Glossary

**A la**
In the style of.

**A la king**
Served in a rich white sauce that usually has mushrooms, green pepper, and pimento in it.

**A la mode**
1) Pie served with ice cream. 2) Beef braised in wine.

**Appetizer**
A light first course of a meal; sometimes it is served with drinks before sitting down to the meal.

**Au gratin**
Dishes with a crusty top usually made with fine breadcrumbs, cheese, and butter.

**Bake**
To cook by dry heat in an oven; called roasting if the food is meat or poultry.

**Barbecue**
To cook food, usually meat, over coals or under the broiler.

**Baste**
To moisten food with a fat or liquid while it is cooking, usually during roasting; melted butter, pan drippings, and sauces are the most common basting substances.

**Batter**
A mixture of flour, fat, liquid, eggs, and sometimes other ingredients; it can be for a cake, cookies, pancakes, or as a coating for fried food.

**Beat**
To mix foods or liquids thoroughly by lifting and turning vigorously with a spoon, fork, wire whisk, hand beater, or electric mixer.

**Blanch**
To plunge food into boiling water for a few minutes until it has softened, or is partially cooked. This is usually done to loosen the skin of fruits or nuts, to whiten or set color of foods, or as a step in preparing vegetables for freezing. Blanching is also done to reduce the strong flavor of such foods as onions, and the saltiness of such foods as smoked bacon.

**Blend**
To mix two or more ingredients until well combined, but not with as vigorous a motion as for beating.

**Bouquet Garni**
A combination of parsley, thyme, and bay leaf used to flavor soups, stews, stocks, and sauces. If fresh herbs are used, they are tied together with the parsley enfolding them; if dried, they are tied in a small piece of cheesecloth or muslin. (Bouquet garni can also be obtained already packaged in small bags like tea bags.) Other herbs are sometimes called for, but they will be specified in a recipe.

**Boil**
To cook food in a boiling liquid, usually water; the liquid will be rolling and sending up bubbles that break at the surface.

**Braise**
To cook food in a small amount of liquid in a covered pan at low temperature, either over

a direct flame or in the oven. Usually food is first browned in fat before braising.

**Bread**
To coat food with breadcrumbs or similar crushed dry ingredients.

**Broil**
To cook food by direct heat, usually *under* the source of heat, doing only one side of the food at a time. (See grill.)

**Brush**
To spread the surface of food thinly with fat, milk, or beaten egg, using a pastry brush, crumpled paper, or cloth.

**Candy**
To cook food, especially carrots and sweet potatoes, in sugar or syrup until coated.

**Caramelize**
To melt sugar in a skillet over low heat until it becomes a golden brown syrup; it must be stirred constantly during the whole cooking process.

**Casserole**
A baked dish containing a combination of meat, seafood, or poultry and vegetables, so called because it is usually cooked in a casserole.

**Chill**
To let food get cold by refrigerating it or placing it in ice or ice water.

**Chop**
To cut food into small pieces.

**Coat**
To cover food all over with flour, crumbs, or batter.

**Cool**
To let food stand at room temperature or in the refrigerator until no longer warm to the touch.

**Coat a spoon**
A test to determine the thickness of a sauce; if a spoon dipped into a sauce comes out with a fairly thick, even coating, the consistency should be right.

**Cream**
To work butter and sugar, and sometimes other ingredients, to a smooth, creamy state, also often described as fluffy, usually by means of a spoon.

**Cube**
1) To cut food into small pieces about ½-inch thick. 2) To tenderize meat by cutting the surface in a diamond or checkered pattern, so breaking tough fibers.

**Cut in**
To combine solid fat and flour or other dry ingredients with a cutting motion, using two knives or a pastry blender, until the fat is fully and evenly coated, and forms particles of the desired size.

**Decant**
1) To pour off a liquid gently so as not to stir up any sediment at the bottom, as in wine or vinegar. 2) To pour a liquid from one bottle to another.

# Glossary (continued)

**Deep fry**
To cook in hot fat that is deep enough to cover the food.

**Deglaze**
To scrape off and cook in added liquid all the degreased bits of cooking juices in the same pan used for roasting or sautéeing meat. This is a step in making meat sauces and gravies.

**Degrease**
1) To remove fat from the surface of hot liquids, such as soup or stock. This is a slow process, best done in three steps. The first is to draw a long-handled spoon over the surface, and to dip up a thin layer of fat while the cooking goes on. The second is to let the liquid settle for five minutes when the cooking is done, and to spoon off the fat that has risen to the top during the settling. (Tipping the pan so that the fat collects at one side makes this easier.) The third is to blot up the last of the fat globules with absorbent paper. If there is time to chill the liquid, degreasing is much easier because the fat will congeal on the top, and can be quickly scraped off. 2) To remove the fat from a roast's pan drippings. This is done by tilting the pan, and removing the fat from the corner with a spoon, both during and after roasting. A tablespoon or so of fat is usually left in the pan to give flavor to the sauce or gravy that will be made.

**Dice**
To cut food into very small cubes, about $\frac{1}{8}$-to-$\frac{1}{4}$-inch in size.

**Dissolve**
To mix a dry ingredient with a liquid until a solution has been formed from the two.

**Dot**
To scatter bits of butter, cheese, or the like over the surface of food, usually before baking or broiling.

**Dredge**
To coat food with a dry ingredient such as flour, cornmeal, or cracker crumbs.

**Fillet**
A lean strip of boneless fish or meat.

**Flake**
To break food into small pieces with a fork.

**Flambé**
To pour brandy, liqueur, or other spirits over food, and set it aflame.

**Fold or fold in**
1) To blend a light and delicate ingredient, such as beaten egg whites or whipped cream, into a heavier mixture, such as a cake batter or pudding base; the proper motion for this is to cut down through the mixture with a spoon or other utensil, to slide it across the bottom of the bowl, and to bring it up and over, turning a part of the heavier mixture on top of the lighter, and repeating the action quickly until the light mixture has been incorporated. 2) To mix in any ingredient without breaking or mashing it—such as heart of artichokes into salad.

**Frizzle**
To panfry until the edges curl, usually bacon and the like.

**Frost**
To cover a cake with frosting; the same as to ice.

**Fry**
To cook food in a small amount of hot fat; usually referred to as sauté, and also called panfry.

**Garnish**
To decorate food with other food, such as parsley on a roast, or rose radishes on a salad.

**Glaze**
To coat food with syrup, sugar syrup, or another edible substance that becomes shiny on cooling.

**Grate**
To break food up into particles by rubbing it on a grater.

**Gravy**
A sauce made with pan drippings of meat or poultry thickened with flour.

**Grease**
To spread fat on the surface of a pan or dish so that the food cooked in it will not stick; often applied to preparing cake pans for use.

**Grill**
To cook food by direct heat, usually *over* the source of heat, doing only one side of the food at a time. (See broil.)

**Grind**
To cut food into small particles with a grinder or blender.

**Ice**
To cover a cake with icing; the same as to frost.

**Knead**
To use a fold-and-press motion with the hands and knuckles to work a dough mixture.

**Lard**
To lay strips of fat over, or put them into the flesh of lean meat, poultry, or fish to give juiciness and flavor in cooking; insertion is done by means of a skewer or a larding needle.

**Liquor**
1) The liquid in which a food has been cooked. 2) The liquid in which a food has been packed.

**Marinade**
A well-flavored liquid, usually of wine or vinegar, oil, and spices, in which food is soaked for a time to make it more flavorful and tender.

**Marinate**
To let food stand in a marinade. This term refers to meat, while the term for fruit is to macerate.

**Melt**
To liquify a food by heating.

**Mince**
To cut food into very fine pieces with a knife, a food grinder, or a blender.

**Pan**
To cook food, mainly vegetables, first in a

small amount of hot fat, then in the steam trapped when a tight cover is quickly clapped on; the food must be shaken frequently while cooking. Sometimes a little liquid is added before covering. Food to be cooked this way must be cut small in uniform pieces.

**Panbroil**
To cook food in a hot frying pan that is either ungreased, lightly greased, or sprinkled with salt, pouring off the fat as it drips out.

**Panfry**
To cook food in a small amount of fat; the same as to fry, or sauté.

**Parboil**
To cook food in boiling liquid until partially tender, in preparation for completing the cooking by another method.

**Pare**
To cut off all or part of the outer coat or layer of a food.

**Peel**
To stip off the skin or rind of a food.

**Pipe**
To decorate with a piping tube.

**Poach**
To cook food in a simmering liquid.

**Pot roast**
To cook large pieces of meat by braising.

**Preheat**
To bring the oven or broiler to the desired the temperature before placing the food in it.

**Purée**
To turn solid food into a pulpy mash, usually by pressing it through a sieve. A blender, ricer, or food mill can also be used.

**Reconstitute**
To restore concentrated food, such as fruit juice or powdered milk, to its natural state, usually by adding water.

**Reduce**
To boil down a liquid so that it is reduced in quantity; this makes its taste more concentrated. Reducing is often a step in making sauces.

**Render**
To remove all connective tissue and possible impurities from fat by melting it slowly, and draining off the liquid.

**Rice**
To press food through a ricer.

**Roast**
To cook by dry heat in an oven; the same as to bake, but applied to meat and poultry.

**Roux**
A paste made by cooking flour and butter together slowly; used as the thickening agent for a sauce or gravy to be cooked in the same pan.

**Sauté**
To cook food in a small amount of hot fat. (See fry, panfry.)

**Scald**
1) To heat a liquid to just below the boiling point, when bubbles form on the surface, but do not break. 2) To dip food in boiling liquid for a short time.

**Scallop**
To bake food that has been sliced, layered, and sauced.

**Score**
To make even, shallow gashes or slits in the surface of food, usually meat or fish; it is done to increase tenderness, or to prevent fat from curling.

**Sear**
To brown the surface of meat quickly at high heat.

**Shred**
To cut food into slivers or thin sticks with a knife or shredder.

**Simmer**
To cook food in liquid at a very slow boil, in which bubbles form slowly and break below the surface.

**Steam**
To cook food by contact with live steam created by placing the food in an inner container over boiling water in a closed pan. Pressure cooking is a steaming method.

**Steep**
To soak in a hot liquid in order to extract flavor or color, or both, as tea or herbs in hot water.

**Stew**
To cook food slowly in simmering liquid, usually in an amount somewhat bigger than for braising.

**Stir**
To mix food with a circular motion; it is best to begin at the center and widen the circle as the ingredients become blended.

**Stir-fry**
To cook food the Chinese way by stirring it quickly and constantly in an uncovered pan over high heat in a small amount of hot oil. Some foods take short additional cooking in a small amount of liquid. All foods must be carefully cut in uniformly small pieces, whether cubed or sliced.

**Toast**
To brown food in dry heat.

**Toss**
To mix food by lifting and dropping lightly with forks or spoons.

**Truss**
To tie meat or poultry with string, or fasten it with skewers, so that it will hold its shape while cooking.

**Try out**
To fry pieces of fat meat, such as bacon, until the membrane is crisp and free of all fat.

**Whip**
To beat rapidly with a wire whisk, beater, or mixer. In whipping, air is incorporated, and volume increased.

# Special Oriental Ingredients

When you go to a store to buy Chinese or Japanese food, it can be helpful to know some of the main ingredients by their original names. This list not only gives such names, but also tells you a little about the food's taste, use, and some possible substitutions. The Chinese and Japanese use many ingredients in common. In these cases, the food is listed under the Chinese name, with the Japanese name included at the end.

## Chinese

**Baak-choy**—cabbage. The Chinese variety is long with smooth white stalks and large green leaves, looking like leaf lettuce. It has a delicate flavor. The Japanese word for the same cabbage is *hakusai.*

**Baak faahn**—cooked rice. This is the staple food in China, as in most Far Eastern countries, and is used as the basis of soups and desserts as well as at almost all meals. The Japanese call it *gohan.*

**Choong**—onion, specifically the green onion, which is the most commonly used.

**Doong gwooh**—dried mushroom. It is brownish-black in color, and has a stronger and more distinctive flavor than fresh mushrooms; it must be soaked before use.

**Dow ngaah**—bean sprouts. The tiny crunchy shoots of the mung bean, used in a great many dishes. The canned variety is not recommended, but if fresh ones are not available, they can be easily grown in the home.

**Fooh jook**—bean curd. This is a custard-like product in the shape of little square cakes, made from puréed soybeans. It is practically pure protein, highly nutritious, and one of the most important ingredients in both Chinese and Japanese cooking. The Japanese word for bean curd is *tofu.*

**Geung**—ginger root. An important flavoring ingredient, used nearly as often as onions and garlic. Because it is sharp in taste, only a little is used at a time. Ground ginger is *not* a substitute. The Japanese call ginger root *shoga.*

**Haw-laahn dow**—young peas still in the pod, and eaten pod and all. Called snow peas or Chinese peas in English.

**Heung new fun**—five-spice powder. A dark brown spice mixture containing star anise, cloves, fennel, anise pepper, and cinnamon. It is very strong and pungent, and used only in small amounts.

**Hoisin**—a thick red sauce that is spicy in taste. Used frequently with shellfish, spareribs, duck, and vegetables.

**Jeung yow**—soy sauce. One of the most widely used ingredients in the Chinese and Japanese cuisines, used both in cooking and as a dip. It is brown in color, and somewhat salty in taste. The Japanese variety, called *shoyu,* is much lighter in flavor.

**Jook sun**—bamboo shoots. The crispy shoots of the bamboo plant, used frequently as a vegetable. Carrot can be substituted for texture, but is not similar in taste. Called *takenoko* in Japanese.

**Mei jing**—monosodium glutamate. A white powder that enhances the flavor of other foods without giving a flavor of its own. Extensively used in all Chinese and Japanese cooking. Known as *aji-no-moto* in Japanese.

## *Japanese*

**Daikon**—white radish. A popular vegetable that grows to giant size, but is sold in sections as small as six inches. White turnip is an acceptable substitute.

**Dashi**—a basic soup and cooking stock made with dried bonito, dried kelp, and water. It is a mainstay of Japanese cooking, both as a clear soup to which various garnishes are added, and as a cooking liquid.

**Goma**—sesame seeds. There are both white and black varieties, which are much-used as a spice. They are usually first warmed and then ground before use. Italian sesame seeds make a good substitute.

**Hichimi togarashi**—seven-pepper spice. A blend of mustard seed, hemp seed, rape seed, poppy seed, pepper leaf, and dried tangerine peel in powdered form. It can range from fairly mild to very hot. Used as a garnish and to season rice and noodle dishes.

**Katsuobushi**—dried bonito. Made by slowly drying the bonito fish, it looks like a hard stick of thin wood, and must be shaved before use. It is an essential ingredient of *dashi*. There is also a preshaved form available.

**Kombu**—dried kelp. The other essential ingredient of *dashi*, this is a species of seaweed that comes in hard black sheets. It is usually cut into short strips for use.

**Miso**—soybean paste. One of the cornerstones of all Japanese cooking. Used in making the traditional breakfast soup, *misoshiru*, in dressings, and as a marinade. The two most used types are *akamiso*, which is red and lightly salted, and *shiromiso*, which is whitish yellow and slightly sweet, although also lightly salted.

**Nori**—dried laver, a species of seaweed. Comes in paper-thin greenish-black sheets. Widely used as a garnish or as a wrapping for rice and rice mixtures.

**Sake**—rice wine. Used as a beverage and in cooking, it usually has the same alcoholic content as sherry. Dry sherry can be substituted for it in cooking.

**Wasabi**—horseradish that becomes green in color in its powdered form which, like dry mustard, must be mixed with water for use. It is also widely used in grated form in dipping sauces.

# For Your Bookshelf

**Contemporary Meal Management**
by Mary Kramer and Margaret Spader, John Wiley & Sons, Inc. (New York: 1972)

**The Joy of Cooking**
by Irma S. Rombauer and Marion R. Becker, Bobbs-Merill Co., Inc. (Indianapolis, Indiana: 1964)

**Food and Man**
by Miriam Lowenberg and Others, John Wiley & Sons, Inc. (New York: 1968)

**Understanding Baking**
by Donald E. Lundberg, Cahners Publishing Co., Inc. (Boston: 1971)

**Food Fundamentals**
by Margaret McWilliams, John Wiley & Sons. Inc. (New York: 1966)

**Chinese Cooking**
by Emily Hahn, Time-Life Books (New York: 1969)

## Picture Credits

Photos and diagrams © Aldus Books (Graeham French) 2, 17–18, 20(T), 21, 25, 27–28, 34–35, 38, 44–45, 48–50, 54–55, 57–81, 86, 87(T), 88, 90–93, 95–99, 101, 102(T)(C), 104, 105(B), 106, 123, 130, 133, (Graeme Harris) 22, (Stuart Stephenson) 11(CR), (Shabtai Tal) 11(BL), (Mary Tomlin) 19, 20(R) 23–24, 26, 29(L), 30, 39–41, 43, 46(B), 47, 53, 122(L); The Bettmann Archive 14(T); British Domestic Appliances 128; Cadbury Typhoo Food Advisory. 107; *Zu Haus* Camera Press, London 4, 32(L), 33(TL)(TR); Colorific! (B. Angove) 7(TR), (Terence Le Goubin) 14(BL), (John Moss) 6(B), 7(TL)(BR), 10(BL), 11(BR), 13(TR)(BL); Editorial Photocolor Archives 12(BL), (D. W. Funt) 7(BL), 9(BR); Electrolux Scandinavia Kitchen Furniture 33(B); Expression Photo Library Ltd. 11(T), 15(TR); FPG (Richard Meek) 14(BR), (W. R. Wilson) 15(TL); Fawcett Publications, Inc. 112–113; By courtesy of General Foods Limited (Chocolate Walnut Gateau) 102(B), (Black Forest Cake, Rice Party Dessert and Vacherin) 103, (Bird's Dream Topping in Pancakes) 105(T); Anthony Howarth/Susan Griggs 12(BR); Guildhall Library, City of London 8(BL); William Cremin/Robert Harding Associates 9(BL); Ted Spiegel/The John Hillelson Agency 13(BR); Pressure cooker and kitchen utensils loaned by John Lewis, London/Photos Graeham French ©Aldus Books 29(R), 31; Mansell Collection 6(T), 8(TR); ©Marshall Cavendish Ltd. 37, 46(T), 51, 84, 85, 110, 111(B), 116, 118, 120–121, 131, 134, (Alan Duns) 87(B), (Roger Phillips) 124–125, 127; Photo Colin Mayer 119; From *Popular Freezer Cookery*, Octopus Books, Ltd., London 135; Picturepoint, London 10(TR)(BR); Radio Times Hulton Picture Library 9(T), 12(T); Syndication International Ltd., London 94; The Tate Gallery, London 8(TL); Transworld 108, 109, 111(T), 114–115, 132; A. Simonsson/ZEFA 15(BR)